Rick S POCKET

LONDON

Rick Steves & Gene Openshaw

P9-DHL-102

Contents

Introduction

Blow through the city on a double-decker bus, and wander the lively West End. Hear the chimes of Big Ben, ogle the crown jewels at the Tower of London, and go for a spin on the London Eye. Visit with Van Gogh in the National Gallery, and rummage through our civilization's attic at the British Museum. Top off your day tipping a pint in a pub with a chatty local.

This is London. It's a city that seems perpetually at your service, with an impressive slate of sights, entertainment, and eateries, all linked by a great transit system. With a growing number of immigrants from all over the world, London has become a city of eight million separate dreams, learning—sometimes fitfully—to live as a microcosm of the once-vast British Empire.

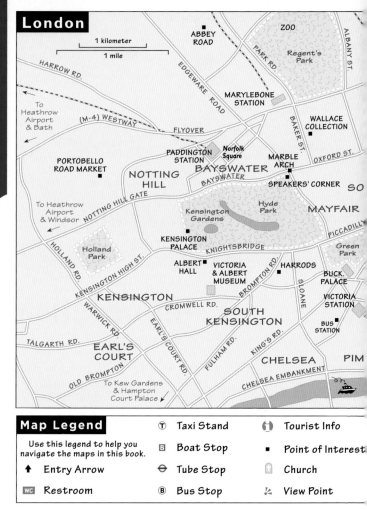

London

1 kilometer

1 mile

ABBEY ROAD

ZOO

Regent's Park

ALBANY ST.

HARROW RD.

EDGEWARE ROAD

PARK RD.

MARYLEBONE STATION

WALLACE COLLECTION

To Heathrow Airport & Bath

(M-4) WESTWAY

FLYOVER

BAKER ST.

PORTOBELLO ROAD MARKET

PADDINGTON STATION

Norfolk Square

MARBLE ARCH

OXFORD ST.

NOTTING HILL

BAYSWATER

BAYSWATER

SPEAKERS' CORNER

SO

To Heathrow Airport & Windsor

NOTTING HILL GATE

Kensington Gardens

Hyde Park

MAYFAIR

PICCADILLY

HOLLAND RD.

Holland Park

KENSINGTON PALACE

KNIGHTSBRIDGE

Green Park

KENSINGTON HIGH ST.

ALBERT HALL

VICTORIA & ALBERT MUSEUM

BROMPTON RD.

HARRODS

BUCK. PALACE

KENSINGTON

CROMWELL RD.

SLOANE

VICTORIA STATION

WARWICK RD.

SOUTH KENSINGTON

BUS STATION

TALGARTH RD.

EARL'S COURT

EARL'S COURT RD.

FULHAM RD.

KING'S RD.

CHELSEA

PIM

OLD BROMPTON

CHELSEA EMBANKMENT

To Kew Gardens & Hampton Court Palace

Map Legend

Use this legend to help you navigate the maps in this book.

♦ Entry Arrow	ⓣ Taxi Stand	👤 Tourist Info
ᴡᴄ Restroom	ⓑ Boat Stop	▪ Point of Interest
	⊖ Tube Stop	🏠 Church
	ⓑ Bus Stop	⅙ View Point

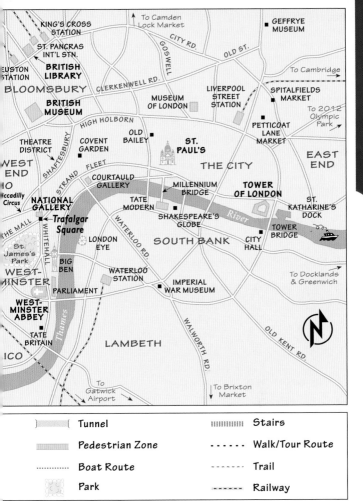

KING'S CROSS STATION
To Camden Lock Market
GEFFRYE MUSEUM
ST. PANCRAS INT'L STN.
CITY RD.
GOSWELL
OLD ST.
EUSTON STATION
BRITISH LIBRARY
BLOOMSBURY
CLERKENWELL RD.
To Cambridge
MUSEUM OF LONDON
LIVERPOOL STREET STATION
SPITALFIELDS MARKET
BRITISH MUSEUM
HIGH HOLBORN
To 2012 Olympic Park
PETTICOAT LANE MARKET
THEATRE DISTRICT
COVENT GARDEN
OLD BAILEY
ST. PAUL'S
EAST END
WEST END
SHAFTESBURY
STRAND
FLEET
THE CITY
HO
Piccadilly Circus
NATIONAL GALLERY
COURTAULD GALLERY
MILLENNIUM BRIDGE
TOWER OF LONDON
ST. KATHARINE'S DOCK
THE MALL
WHITEHALL
Trafalgar Square
TATE MODERN
SHAKESPEARE'S GLOBE
River
TOWER BRIDGE
St. James's Park
LONDON EYE
WATERLOO RD.
SOUTH BANK
CITY HALL
BIG BEN
To Docklands & Greenwich
WEST-MINSTER
PARLIAMENT
WATERLOO STATION
IMPERIAL WAR MUSEUM
WEST-MINSTER ABBEY
Thames
WALWORTH RD.
OLD KENT RD.
TATE BRITAIN
LAMBETH
N
ICO
To Gatwick Airport
To Brixton Market

	Tunnel		Stairs
	Pedestrian Zone	.....	Walk/Tour Route
....	Boat Route	------	Trail
	Park	-------	Railway

About This Book

With this book, I've selected only the best of London—admittedly, a tough call. The core of the book is eight self-guided tours. These zero in on London's greatest sights, from a Westminster Walk past #10 Downing Street, to the treasures of the British Library, to the top of St. Paul's 365-foot dome. The rest of the book is a traveler's tool kit. You'll find hints on saving money, avoiding crowds, getting around London, finding a great meal, and more.

London—A City of Neighborhoods

London, with more than 600 square miles and eight million people, is a world in itself. On my first visit, I felt extremely small.

The Thames River runs roughly west to east through the city, with most of the visitor's sights on the north bank. Think of London as a collection of neighborhoods:

Central London: The heart of today's London contains the Westminster district (Big Ben, the Abbey, and #10 Downing Street) and the West End (Piccadilly Circus, theaters, restaurants, and nightlife). In the middle sits London's gathering place, Trafalgar Square.

Key to Symbols

Sights are rated:

▲▲▲ Don't miss
▲▲ Try hard to see
▲ Worthwhile if you can make it
No rating Worth knowing about

For opening times, if a sight is listed as "May–Oct daily 9:00–16:00," it's open from 9 A.M. until 4 P.M. from the first day of May until the last day of October.

If you'd like more information than this Pocket Guide offers, I've sprinkled the book liberally with web references, including my own website. For updates to this book, feedback from fellow travelers, in-depth travel tips, and much more, visit **www.ricksteves.com**.

London's Neighborhoods

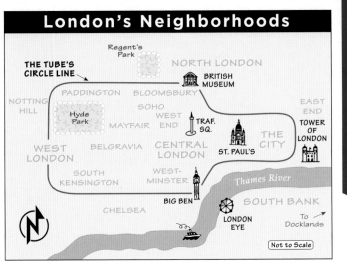

The City: Surrounding St. Paul's Cathedral is the former walled city of Shakespeare's day. Now it's the modern financial district, called simply "The City." On its eastern border stands the Tower of London.

West London: This huge area surrounding the green expanse of Hyde Park/Kensington Gardens contains upscale neighborhoods such as Mayfair, Belgravia, Chelsea, South Kensington, and Notting Hill. Here you'll find a range of sights (Victoria and Albert Museum, Tate Britain, Harrods) and my top hotel recommendations.

North London: This contains the British Museum, the British Library, and the overhyped Madame Tussauds Waxworks, as well as three major train stations.

The South Bank: The Thames' south bank offers major sights (Shakespeare's Globe, Tate Modern, London Eye) and minor attractions, all linked by a riverside walkway.

East London: East of The City is the once-grimy, increasingly gentrified East End. Even farther are the skyscraper-filled Docklands and Canary Wharf, plus Olympic Park—all newly developed areas signaling London's future.

London at a Glance

Introduction

▲▲▲**Westminster Abbey** Britain's finest church and the site of royal coronations and burials since 1066. **Hours:** Mon–Fri 9:30–16:30, Wed until 19:00, Sat 9:30–14:30, closed Sun to sightseers except for worship. See page 29.

▲▲▲**Churchill War Rooms** Underground WWII headquarters of Churchill's war effort. **Hours:** Daily 9:30–18:00. See page 142.

▲▲▲**National Gallery** Remarkable collection of European paintings (1250–1900), including Leonardo, Botticelli, Velázquez, Rembrandt, Turner, Van Gogh, and the Impressionists. **Hours:** Daily 10:00–18:00, Fri until 21:00. See page 39.

▲▲▲**British Museum** The world's greatest collection of artifacts of Western civilization, including the Rosetta Stone and the Parthenon's Elgin Marbles. **Hours:** Daily 10:00–17:30, Fri until 20:30, but not all galleries open after 17:30. See page 75.

▲▲▲**British Library** Impressive collection of the most important literary treasures of the Western world. **Hours:** Mon–Fri 9:30–18:00, Tue until 20:00, Sat 9:30–17:00, Sun 11:00–17:00. See page 103.

▲▲▲**St. Paul's Cathedral** The main cathedral of the Anglican Church, designed by Christopher Wren, with a climbable dome and daily even-song services. **Hours:** Mon–Sat 8:30–16:30, dome opens at 9:30, closed Sun except for worship. See page 115.

▲▲▲**Tower of London** Historic castle, palace, and prison housing the crown jewels and a witty band of Beefeaters. **Hours:** March–Oct Tue–Sat 9:00–17:30, Sun–Mon 10:00–17:30; Nov–Feb Tue–Sat 9:00–16:30, Sun–Mon 10:00–16:30. See page 127.

▲▲▲**Victoria and Albert Museum** The best collection of decorative arts anywhere. **Hours:** Daily 10:00–17:45, Fri until 22:00 (selected galleries). See page 170.

▲▲**London Eye** Enormous observation wheel, offering commanding views over London's skyline. **Hours:** Daily July–Aug 10:00–21:30, April–June 10:00–21:00, Sept–March 10:00–20:00. See page 161.

▲▲**Tate Modern** Works by Monet, Matisse, Dalí, Picasso, and Warhol displayed in a converted powerhouse. **Hours:** Daily 10:00–18:00, Fri–Sat until 22:00. See page 164.

▲▲**Big Ben and Houses of Parliament** London's famous Neo-Gothic landmark, topped by Big Ben and occupied by the Houses of Lords and Commons. **Hours** (both Houses): Generally Mon–Tue 14:30–22:00, Wed 11:30–22:00, Thu 10:30–19:00, Sat by guided tour only, closed Fri and Sun and most of Aug–Sept. See page 142.

▲▲**National Portrait Gallery** A *Who's Who* of British history, featuring portraits of this nation's most important historical figures. **Hours:** Daily 10:00–18:00, Thu–Fri until 21:00, first and second floors open Mon at 11:00. See page 144.

▲▲**Imperial War Museum** Examines the military history of the bloody 20th century. **Hours:** Daily 10:00–18:00. See page 162.

▲▲**Shakespeare's Globe** Timbered, thatched-roofed reconstruction of the Bard's original wooden "O." **Hours:** Theater complex, museum, and actor-led tours generally daily 9:00–17:00; in summer, morning theater tours only. Plays are also staged here. See page 165.

▲▲**Tate Britain** Collection of British painting from the 16th century through modern times, including works by William Blake, the Pre-Raphaelites, and J. M. W. Turner. **Hours:** Daily 10:00–18:00, some Fri until 22:00. See page 168.

▲▲**Buckingham Palace** Britain's royal residence with the famous Changing of the Guard. **Hours:** Palace—Aug–Sept only, daily 9:30–18:30; Guard—generally May–July daily at 11:30, Aug–April every other day. See page 148.

▲▲**Kensington Palace** Recently restored former home of British monarchs, with appealing exhibits on Queen Victoria, as well as William and Mary. **Hours:** Daily 10:00–18:00, until 17:00 Nov–Feb. See page 171.

▲▲**Natural History Museum** Packed with stuffed creatures, engaging exhibits, and enthralled kids. **Hours:** Daily 10:00–17:50. See page 170.

▲**Courtauld Gallery** Fine collection of paintings filling one wing of the Somerset House, a grand 18th-century palace. **Hours:** Daily 10:00–18:00. See page 148.

Daily Reminder

Sunday: The Tower of London and British Museum are both especially crowded today. These places are closed: Houses of Parliament, Banqueting House, Sir John Soane's Museum, City Hall, and Old Bailey. Westminster Abbey and St. Paul's are open during the day for worship but closed to sightseers. The neighborhood called The City is dead. Sunday morning is a good time to take a bus tour. The Speakers' Corner in Hyde Park rants all afternoon. Most big stores are open 12:00–18:00. Street markets flourish at Camden Lock, Spitalfields, and Greenwich, but Portobello Road is closed. Most theaters (except maybe *The Lion King* and Shakespeare's Globe) are dark.

Monday: Virtually all sights are open except for Apsley House, Sir John Soane's Museum, Vinopolis, and a few others. The Courtauld Gallery is free until 14:00. The Houses of Parliament may be open (when in session) as late as 22:00.

Tuesday: Virtually all sights are open, except for Apsley House and Vinopolis. The British Library is open until 20:00. On the first Tuesday of the month, Sir John Soane's Museum is also open 18:00–21:00. The Houses of Parliament may be open (when in session) as late as 22:00.

Wednesday: Virtually all sights are open. The Houses of Parliament may be open as late as 22:00.

Thursday: All sights are open, plus evening hours at the National Portrait Gallery (until 21:00) and Vinopolis (until 21:30).

Friday: All sights are open, except the Houses of Parliament. Sights open late include the British Museum (selected galleries until 20:30), National Gallery (until 21:00), National Portrait Gallery (until 21:00), Vinopolis (until 21:30), Victoria and Albert Museum (selected galleries until 22:00), and Tate Modern (until 22:00). The Tate Britain is sometimes open late on select Fridays.

Saturday: Most sights are open except Old Bailey, City Hall, and Houses of Parliament (except with a tour). Skip The City. Vinopolis is open until 21:30 and the Tate Modern until 22:00. The Portobello Road, Camden Lock, and Greenwich markets are good today.

Planning Your Time

The following day-plans give an idea of how much an organized, motivated, and caffeinated person can see. Begin with the Day 1 plan—the most important sights—and add on from there.

Day 1: Start where London did, at the 950-year-old Tower of London, with its crown jewels, blustery Beefeaters, and bloody history. Then pack a picnic lunch and cruise the Thames to Westminster Abbey; tour it and stay for the evensong. Then follow my self-guided Westminster Walk, ending with dinner in the West End.

Day 2: Take a London sightseeing bus tour and hop off at Buckingham Palace for the Changing of the Guard. After lunch, tour the Cabinet War Rooms and Churchill Museum, and then the National Gallery. Have a pub dinner before a play, concert, or evening walking tour.

Day 3: Tour the British Museum, then have lunch. Tube to Leicester Square to take my self-guided West End Walk: see Covent Garden and Soho, and browse the Regent Street shops. Enjoy afternoon tea at Fortnum & Mason or The Wolseley.

Day 4: Walk through The City and take the St. Paul's Tour. Cross the Millennium Bridge to the South Bank of the Thames. Tour Shakespeare's Globe, the Tate Modern, and nearby sights. Then stroll the Jubilee Walkway to the London Eye.

Day 5: Explore a morning street market, especially Saturday at Portobello Road or Sunday at Spitalfields. Then choose from other major sights: the British Library, Tate Britain, Museum of London, Imperial War Museum, or Kew Gardens.

Day 6: Tour the Victoria and Albert Museum, and/or its neighboring museums. Spend the afternoon strolling through Hyde Park or shopping at Harrods or other venues.

Day 7: Consider a day trip outside the city—a cruise to salty Greenwich, Hampton Palace, or Windsor Castle, or a visit to the Docklands and Olympic Park.

With More Time: Spend a day or two on side-trips to Cambridge, Stonehenge, or Bath.

These are busy day-plans, so be sure to schedule in slack time for laundry, people-watching, shopping, snafus, and recharging your touristic batteries.

Here are a few quick sightseeing tips to get you started. Master London's excellent public transportation system, and buy the right pass to make it economical. Use the "Daily Reminder" to visit sights at their most opportune time. Follow my tips on avoiding lines and crowds. Take advantage of the free Rick Steves audio tours, covering many of this book's sights. Budget time and energy for London after dark. Dine well at least once.

And finally, keep in mind that London is more than its museums and landmarks. It's a living, breathing, thriving organism...a coral reef of humanity. Slow down and be open to unexpected experiences and the friendliness of the British people.

As you visit places I know and love, I'm happy you'll be meeting my favorite Londoners. Cheers!

Westminster Walk

From Big Ben to Trafalgar Square

Just about every visitor to London strolls along historic Whitehall from Big Ben to Trafalgar Square. Under London's modern traffic and big-city bustle lie 2,000 fascinating years of history. This quick nine-stop walk gives meaning to that touristy ramble.

As London's political center, the Westminster neighborhood is both historic and contemporary. See the River Thames where London was born. Pass statues and monuments to the nation's great heroes. Admire the Halls of Parliament where Britain is ruled today, and take a peek at #10 Downing Street, home of the prime minister. All in about an hour.

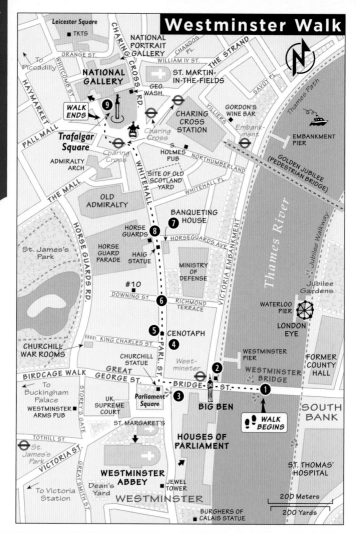

Westminster Walk

Leicester Square
■ TKTS

NATIONAL
PORTRAIT
GALLERY

CHANDOS
PL.

THE STRAND

CHARING CROSS RD.

ORANGE ST.

WILLIAM IV ST.

WHITCOMB ST.

To
Piccadilly

HAYMARKET

**NATIONAL
GALLERY**

GEO.
WASH.

ST. MARTIN-
IN-THE-FIELDS

SAVOY PL.

Thames Path

**WALK
ENDS** ❾

CHARING
CROSS
STATION

GORDON'S
WINE BAR

Embankment

EMBANKMENT
PIER

PALL MALL

**Trafalgar
Square**

Charing
Cross

VILLIERS

GOLDEN JUBILEE (PEDESTRIAN BRIDGE)

Charing
Cross

HOLMES
PUB

NORTHUMBERLAND

ADMIRALTY
ARCH

WHITEHALL

S.

SITE OF OLD
SCOTLAND
YARD

WHITEHALL PL.

Thames River

THE MALL

OLD
ADMIRALTY

BANQUETING
HOUSE ❼

HORSE GUARDS RD.

St. James's
Park

HORSE
GUARDS ❽

HORSEGUARDS AVE.

VICTORIA EMBANKMENT

Jubilee Walkway

HORSE
GUARD
PARADE

HAIG
STATUE

MINISTRY
OF
DEFENSE

Jubilee
Gardens

#10

DOWNING ST.

❻

RICHMOND
TERRACE

WATERLOO
PIER

LONDON
EYE

CHURCHILL
WAR ROOMS

❺

KING CHARLES ST.

CENOTAPH

PARL. ST.

BIRDCAGE WALK

CHURCHILL
STATUE

GREAT
GEORGE ST.

West-
minster

WESTMINSTER
PIER

WESTMINSTER
BRIDGE

FORMER
COUNTY
HALL

To
Buckingham
Palace

WESTMINSTER
ARMS PUB

STOREY'S GATE

UK
SUPREME
COURT

Parliament
Square

❸

BRIDGE ST.

❷

❶

**WALK
BEGINS**

SOUTH
BANK

ST. MARGARET'S

BIG BEN

TOTHILL ST.

St.
James's
Park

VICTORIA ST.

GREAT SMITH ST.

**WESTMINSTER
ABBEY**

HOUSES OF
PARLIAMENT

To
Victoria
Station

Dean's
Yard

JEWEL
TOWER

ST. THOMAS'
HOSPITAL

WESTMINSTER

200 Meters

200 Yards

BURGHERS OF
CALAIS STATUE

1. Westminster Bridge
2. Statue of Boadicea
3. View of Parliament Square
4. Walking Along Whitehall
5. Cenotaph
6. #10 Downing Street & Ministry of Defense
7. Banqueting House
8. Horse Guards
9. Trafalgar Square

ORIENTATION

Length of This Walk: Allow one hour for a leisurely walk, plus more if you go inside sights along the way.

Getting There: Tube: Westminster, then take the Westminster Pier exit to Westminster Bridge.

WCs: Westminster Pier (50p); at the intersection of Bridge Street and Whitehall (underground, 50p); and free WCs inside the Banqueting House, National Gallery, and St. Martin-in-the-Fields church.

Free Audio Tour: You can download a free Rick Steves audio tour of this chapter, either from iTunes, Google Play, or at www.ricksteves .com.

THE WALK BEGINS

▶ *Start halfway across Westminster Bridge. Look upstream, toward Parliament.*

❶ On Westminster Bridge

Big Ben and the Houses of Parliament: Ding dong ding dong. Dong ding ding dong. Yes, indeed, you are in London.

Big Ben is actually "not the clock, not the tower, but the bell that tolls the hour." However, since the 13-ton bell is not visible, everyone just calls the whole works Big Ben. Named for a fat bureaucrat, Ben is scarcely older than my great-grandmother, but it has quickly become the city's symbol. The tower is 315 feet high, and the clock faces are 23 feet across. The 13-foot-long minute hand sweeps the length of your body every five minutes. For fun, call home (a few pay phones are in the area) at about three minutes before the hour, to let your loved one hear Big Ben ring.

Big Ben is in the north tower of the Houses of Parliament, stretching

Big Ben

Thames cruises

along the Thames. Britain is ruled from this building, as it has been since 1090. Back then, Westminster Palace was the royal palace, the home of the king and queen. Then, as democracy was foisted on tyrants, a parliament of nobles was allowed to meet in some of the rooms. Soon, commoners were elected to office, the neighborhood was shot, and the royalty moved to Buckingham Palace. In 1834, the building was gutted by fire and rebuilt in the sandstone-hued, Neo-Gothic Parliament building we see today.

Today, the House of Commons, which is more powerful than the Queen and prime minister combined, meets in one end of the building. The rubber-stamp House of Lords grumbles and snoozes in the other end of this 1,000-room complex, and provides a tempering effect on extreme governmental changes. The two bickering houses even have separate tea rooms along the river—red awnings for lords, green for commoners. If a flag is flying from the Victoria Tower, at the far south end of the building, Parliament is in session. The modern Portcullis Building (with the tube-like chimneys), across Bridge Street from Big Ben, holds offices for the 659 members of the House of Commons. They commute to the Houses of Parliament by way of an underground passage.

The Thames: London's history is tied to the Thames, the 210-mile river linking the interior of England with the North Sea. The city got its start in Roman times as a trade center along this watery highway. As recently as a century ago, large ships made their way upstream to the city center to unload. Today, the major port is 25 miles downstream, and the massive Thames Barrier (12 miles downstream, built in 1984) keeps the river from flooding at high tide.

Several tour-boat companies offer regular departures from Westminster Pier (on the left bank) or Waterloo Pier (on the right, near the London Eye). This is an efficient, scenic way to get to the Tower of London or Greenwich (downstream) or Kew Gardens (upstream).

For centuries, only London Bridge crossed the Thames. Then in 1750 Westminster Bridge was built. Early in the morning of September 3, 1802, William Wordsworth stood where you're standing and described what he saw:

> *This City now doth, like a garment, wear*
> *The beauty of the morning; silent, bare,*
> *Ships, towers, domes, theatres, and temples lie*
> *Open unto the fields, and to the sky;*
> *All bright and glittering in the smokeless air.*

You'll notice the **London Eye** on the South Bank, across the river.

London Eye

Originally nicknamed "the London Eyesore," it's now generally appreciated by locals, who see it as a welcome addition to their city's otherwise underwhelming skyline. Next to the wheel sprawls a carnival-like tourist complex. The London Eye marks the start of the Jubilee Walkway, a pleasant one-hour promenade along the vibrant, gentrified South Bank, with great views across the river.

▶ *Near Westminster Pier is a big statue of a lady on a chariot (nicknamed "the first woman driver"...no reins).*

❷ Statue of Boadicea, Queen of the Iceni

Riding in her two-horse chariot, daughters by her side, this Celtic Xena leads her people against Roman invaders. Julius Caesar was the first Roman to cross the Channel, but even he was weirded out by the island's strange inhabitants, who worshipped trees, sacrificed virgins, and went to war painted blue.

Boadicea refused to be Romanized. In A.D. 60, after Roman soldiers raped her daughters, she rallied her people and massacred 60,000 Roman sympathizers. However, the brief revolt was snuffed out, and she and her family took poison rather than surrender. The Romans civilized the Celts, building roads and making this spot on the Thames—"Londinium"—into a major urban center.

▶ *Cross the street to just under Big Ben and continue one block inland to the busy intersection of Parliament Square.*

❸ View of Parliament Square

To your left is the **entrance to the Houses of Parliament**, located midway down the building. If Parliament is in session, the entrance is lined with

Boadicea—the Celts' final hurrah

Nelson Mandela in Parliament Square

tourists, enlivened by political demonstrations, and staked out by camera crews interviewing Members of Parliament (MPs) for the evening news.

Kitty-corner across the square, the two white towers of **Westminster Abbey** rise above the trees. The cute little church with the blue sundials, snuggling under the Abbey "like a baby lamb under a ewe," is **St. Margaret's Church.** Since 1480, this has been *the* place for weddings of politicians, including Winston Churchill.

Parliament Square, the expanse of green between Westminster Abbey and Big Ben, is filled with (protesters and) statues of famous Brits such as **Winston Churchill,** the man who saved Britain from Hitler. According to tour guides, the statue has a current of electricity running through it to honor Churchill's wish that his head wouldn't be soiled by pigeons. A few non-Brits are honored for their contributions to mankind. **Nelson Mandela** (at the opposite corner of the square) battled South African apartheid, and **Abraham Lincoln** (far side of the square) opposed apartheid in America. The Lincoln statue, erected in 1920, was patterned after a similar statue in Chicago's Lincoln Park.

The broad boulevard of **Whitehall** (here called Parliament Street) stretches to your right up to Trafalgar Square. In 1868, this intersection became the site of a new innovation—the world's first traffic light.

▸ *Consider touring Westminster Abbey (❂ see the Westminster Abbey Tour on page 29). Otherwise, turn right (north), and walk up Parliament Street, which becomes Whitehall.*

❹ Walking Along Whitehall

Today, Whitehall is choked with traffic, but imagine the effect this broad street must have had on out-of-towners a century ago. In your horse-drawn carriage, you'd clop along a tree-lined boulevard—past well-dressed lords and ladies, dodging street urchins—your eyes dazzled by the bone-white walls of this man-made marble canyon.

Whitehall is now the most important street in Britain, lined with the ministries of finance, treasury, and the home of the prime minister. You may see limos and camera crews as important dignitaries enter or exit. Political demonstrators wave signs and chant slogans—sometimes about issues foreign to most Americans, concerning Britain's former colonies that still resent the empire's influence.

Notice the security measures. Iron grates seal off the concrete ditches between the buildings and sidewalks for protection against explosives.

Whitehall's government offices and monuments

Cenotaph—grim reminder of two World Wars

The city has been a target of terrorist attacks since long before September 2001, and Londoners take threats in stride.

▸ *Continue toward the tall, square, concrete monument in the middle of the road—the Cenotaph.*

On your right is a colorful pub, the Red Lion. Across the street, a 700-foot detour down King Charles Street leads to the Churchill War Rooms, the underground bunker of 27 rooms that was the nerve center of Britain's campaign against Hitler.

❺ Cenotaph

This big, white stone monument (in the middle of the boulevard) honors those who died in the two events that most shaped modern Britain—World Wars I and II. The monumental devastation of these wars helped turn a colonial superpower into a cultural colony of an American superpower.

The actual cenotaph is the slab that sits atop the pillar—a tomb. You'll notice no religious symbols on this memorial. The dead honored here came from many creeds and all corners of Britain's empire. It looks lost in a sea of noisy cars, but on each Remembrance Sunday (closest to November 11), Whitehall is closed off to traffic, the royal family fills the balcony overhead in the foreign ministry, and a memorial service is held around the cenotaph.

It's hard for an American to understand the impact of World War I on Europe (1914-1918). Britain lost as many as 20,000 men in a single day. It's said that if the roughly one million WWI dead from the British Empire were to march four abreast past the cenotaph, the sad parade would last for seven days.

▶ *Just past the cenotaph, on the west side of Whitehall, is an iron security gate guarding the entrance to Downing Street.*

❻ #10 Downing Street and the Ministry of Defense

Britain's version of the White House is where the prime minister and his family live, at #10. It's in the black-brick building 300 feet down the blocked-off street, on the right; there's a lantern and usually a security guard.

Like the White House's Rose Garden, the black door marked #10 is a highly symbolic point of power, popular for photo ops to mark big occasions. This is where suffragettes protested in the early 20th century, where Neville Chamberlain showed off his regrettable peace treaty with Hitler, and where Winston Churchill made famous the V-for-Victory sign. In 2008, then Prime Minister Gordon Brown and US President George W. Bush posed here to bolster US–UK solidarity, and in 2009, US President Barack Obama huddled here with Brown to consider solutions to the economic downturn. In 2012 Prime Minister David Cameron posed here to celebrate the Queen's Jubilee and the Olympic Games.

It looks modest, but #10's entryway does open up into fairly impressive digs—the prime minister's offices (downstairs), his residence (upstairs), and two large formal dining rooms. The PM's staff has offices here, and other colleagues are next door at #11 and #12. Many on the staff are permanent bureaucrats, staying on to serve as prime ministers come and go. The cabinet meets at #10 on Tuesday mornings. This is where foreign dignitaries are wined and dined, where the prime minister receives honored school kids and victorious soccer teams, and where he gives monthly addresses to the nation.

This has been the traditional home of the prime minister since the

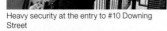

Heavy security at the entry to #10 Downing Street

Memorial to WWII women

Prime Minister David Cameron

David Cameron lives at #10 Downing Street with his wife, Samantha, and their four young children. He heads the Conservative Party (the "Tories"), which came to power in 2010.

The prime minister is not elected directly by popular vote (the way the American president is), but rules as leader of the party that garners the most votes in Parliamentary elections. In 2010, three parties split the vote, forcing Cameron to form a coalition with the more left-leaning Liberal Democrat Party. The Labour Party, which had held power in Britain for 13 years under Gordon Brown and Tony Blair, is the coalition's chief opposition.

Cameron is a moderate Conservative—socially "liberal" (pro gay rights and decriminalization of drugs) and fiscally conservative. His government advocates severe budget cuts to combat Britain's economic recession.

Though "Dave" projects an everyman persona, he was born rich, married rich, and was schooled at Eton (England's most exclusive prep school) and Oxford. The Mayor of London, Boris Johnson, is an old Oxford frat buddy and also a distant cousin. As the Conservatives try to solve Britain's severe economic and cultural problems, it remains to be seen whether David Cameron has brought a fresh enough approach to #10.

position was created in the early 18th century. But even before that, the neighborhood (if not the building itself) was a center of power, where Edward the Confessor and Henry VIII had palaces. The facade is, frankly, quite cheap, having been built as part of a middle-class cul-de-sac of homes by American-born George Downing in the 1680s. When the first PM moved in, the humble interior was combined with a mansion in back. During a major upgrade in the 1950s, they discovered that the facade's black bricks were actually yellow—but had been stained by centuries of Industrial Age soot. To keep with tradition, they now paint the bricks black.

The guarded metal gates were installed in 1989 to protect against Irish terrorists. Even so, #10 was hit and partly damaged in 1991 by an

Irish Republican Army mortar launched from a van. These days, there's typically not much to see unless a VIP happens to drive up. Then the bobbies snap to and check credentials, the gates open, the car is inspected for bombs, the traffic barrier midway down the street drops into its bat cave, the car drives in, and...the bobbies go back to mugging for the tourists.

The huge building across Whitehall from Downing Street is the **Ministry of Defense** (MOD), the "British Pentagon." This bleak place looks like a Ministry of Defense should. In front, statues honor illustrious defenders of Britain, including **Field Marshal Bernard Law Montgomery ("Monty")** who beat the Nazis in North Africa. In 2005, a **memorial** honoring the women who fought and died in World War II was constructed.

You may be enjoying the shade of London's **plane trees.** Their bark sheds and regenerates, which helps them survive in polluted London.

▶ *Continue up Whitehall to the equestrian statue in the middle of the street. On the right side of Whitehall is the Banqueting House.*

❼ Banqueting House

This two-story building is just about all that remains of what was once the biggest palace in Europe—Whitehall Palace, stretching from Trafalgar Square to Big Ben. Henry VIII started the building, and Queen Elizabeth I and other monarchs added on as England's worldwide prestige grew. Then in 1698, a massive fire destroyed Whitehall Palace, leaving only its former dining hall, the Banqueting House.

Today, the exterior of Greek-style columns and pediments looks rather ho-hum, much like every other white, marble building in London. Built in 1620 by architect Inigo Jones, it was the first of its kind, rising above

Banqueting House—Neoclassical trendsetter

Horse Guard manning a symbolic checkpoint

half-timbered thatched buildings. Within a century, London was awash in Georgian-style architecture, the English version of Neoclassical.

The Banqueting House was the site of one of the pivotal events of English history. On January 30, 1649, a man dressed in black stepped out one of the windows and onto a wooden platform. It was King Charles I. He gave a short speech to a huge crowd assembled outside. Then he knelt and laid his neck on a block as another man in black approached. It was the executioner—who cut off the King's head. Plop—the concept of divine monarchy in Britain was decapitated. Though the monarchy was restored a generation later, every ruler since then knows that the monarchy reigns by the grace of Parliament.

▶ *If you're interested in touring the impressive Banqueting House interior, ✪ see page 143. Otherwise, continue up Whitehall on the left (west) side, where you'll see (and smell) the building known as Horse Guards, guarded by traditionally dressed soldiers who are also called Horse Guards.*

❽ Horse Guards

For 200 years, soldiers in cavalry uniforms have guarded this arched entrance along Whitehall. Back when the archway was the only access point to The Mall (the street leading to Buckingham Palace), it was a crucial security checkpoint. By tradition, it's still guarded with much pomp and fanfare.

Two different squads alternate, so depending on the day you visit, you'll see soldiers in either red coats with white plumes in their helmets (the Life Guards), or blue coats with red plumes (the Blues and Royals). Together, they constitute the Queen's personal bodyguard. Besides their ceremonial duties here in old-time uniforms, these elite troops have fought in Iraq and Afghanistan. Both Prince William and Prince Harry have served in the Blues and Royals.

The Horse Guards building was the headquarters of the British army from the time of the American Revolution until the Ministry of Defense was created in World War II. Through the arch is the broad expanse of Horse Guards Parade, where the 2012 Olympics beach volleyball event was held (Changing of the Guard Mon–Sat at 11:00, Sun at 10:00, dismounting ceremony daily at 16:00; the Horse Guards Museum offers a glimpse at the stables and a collection of uniforms and weapons).

▶ *Continue up Whitehall, passing the Old Admiralty (#26, on left), headquarters of the British navy that once ruled the waves. Across the street, behind the old Clarence Pub, stood the original Scotland Yard, headquarters of London's crack police force in the days of Sherlock Holmes. Finally, Whitehall opens up into the grand urban space that is Trafalgar Square.*

❾ Trafalgar Square

London's Times Square bustles around the world's biggest Corinthian column, where **Admiral Horatio Nelson** stands 170 feet tall, looking over London in the direction of one of the greatest naval battles in history. Nelson saved England at a time as dark as World War II. In 1805, Napoleon was poised on the other side of the Channel, threatening to

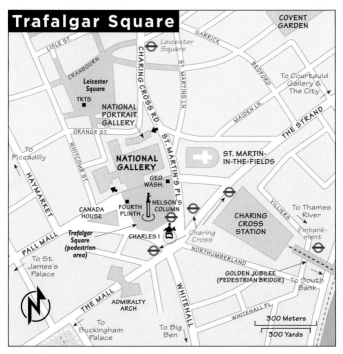

Looking from Trafalgar Square down Whitehall

invade England. Meanwhile, more than 900 miles away, the one-armed, one-eyed, and one-minded Lord Nelson attacked the French fleet off the coast of Spain at Trafalgar. The French were routed, Britannia ruled the waves, and the once-invincible French army was slowly worn down, then defeated at Waterloo. Nelson, while victorious, was shot by a sniper in the battle. He died, gasping, "Thank God, I have done my duty."

At the base of Nelson's column are bronze reliefs cast from melted-down enemy cannons, and four huggable lions dying to have their photo taken with you. In front of the column is a statue of Charles I on horseback, with his head still on his shoulders. In the pavement just behind the statue is a plaque marking the center of London, from which all distances are measured. Of the many statues that dot the square, the pedestal on the northwest corner (the "fourth plinth") is periodically topped with contemporary art. The newly restored fountains, lit by colored lights, can shoot water 80 feet in the air. At the top of Trafalgar Square (north) sits the domed **National Gallery** with its grand staircase, and, to the right, the steeple of **St. Martin-in-the-Fields,** built in 1722, inspiring the steeple-over-the-entrance style of many town churches in New England.

Trafalgar Square is indeed the center of modern London, connecting Westminster, The City, and the West End. Spin clockwise 360 degrees and survey the city:

- Westminster is to the south, with Buckingham Palace to the southwest down the broad boulevard called The Mall.

- Leicester Square, Piccadilly Circus, and Soho are a few blocks north-northwest of Trafalgar Square.

- The area called The City—London's oldest section and today's financial district—is a mile northeast of Trafalgar Square, up the boulevard called the Strand.

- And finally, Northumberland Street leads southeast to the Golden Jubilee pedestrian bridge over the Thames.

Soak it in. You're smack-dab in the center of London, a city thriving atop two millennia of history.

Westminster Abbey Tour

Westminster Abbey is the greatest church in the English-speaking world, where the nation's kings and queens have been crowned and buried since 1066. The histories of Westminster Abbey and England are almost the same. A thousand years of English history (and 3,000 tombs) lie within its stained-glass splendor and under its stone slabs.

On this hour-plus walk, we'll stroll through the elaborate Gothic architecture of the church and see some of England's dearly departed, including the tombs of 29 kings and queens. We'll see memorials to England's greatest politicians, scientists, writers, and warriors. And—in the heart of the church—we'll visit the spot where, one fine day, Prince Charles (or William or Harry) will be crowned the next King of England.

ORIENTATION

Cost: £18, £36 family ticket (2 adults and 1 child), includes fine audioguide and entry to the cloisters and Abbey Museum.

Hours: Abbey—Mon–Fri 9:30–16:30, Wed until 19:00 (main church only), Sat 9:30–14:30, last entry one hour before closing, closed Sun to sightseers but open for services; Abbey Museum—daily 10:30–16:00; cloisters—daily 8:00–18:00.

Avoiding Lines: The Abbey is especially crowded midmorning, and all day Sat and Mon. Visit early, during lunch, or after 14:30 (then stay for the 17:00 evensong). At the ticket-buying line, the "cash" queue moves faster than the "credit" one.

Dress Code: There is none, even for services.

Getting There: Near Big Ben and the Houses of Parliament (Tube: Westminster or St. James's Park).

Information: Because special events can shut out sightseers, check the website or call ahead for the latest on opening hours, concerts, and services. Inside the cathedral, the red-cloaked marshals and green-cloaked vergers are there to help. Tel. 020/7654-4834, www.westminster-abbey.org.

Music and Services: Mon–Fri—7:30 prayer, 8:00 communion, 12:30 communion, 17:00 evensong (may be spoken on Wed); Sat and Sun evensong at 15:00 (except June–Sept, when it's 17:00 on Sat); full day of services on Sun—see website. Praying is always free, thank God, but you can't sightsee. Free organ recitals are often held Sun at 17:45.

Tours: The included audioguide is excellent. Entertaining 90-minute, £3 guided tours leave about every 90 minutes from the entrance.

WCs: Inside the Abbey, WCs are located near Poets' Corner. The nearest public WCs (50p) are in front of Methodist Central Hall, the domed building across the street from the Abbey's west entrance.

Photography: Photos are prohibited.

Cuisine Art: There's a café in the solarium; enter through the cloisters. Find cafeteria-style lunches at Wesley's Café inside Methodist Central Hall (daily 9:00–16:00). The Westminster Arms pub (£9 fish and chips, food served daily 12:00–20:00) is near Methodist Central Hall on Storey's Gate. Picnickers can find benches at the nearby Jewel Tower, a half-block south of the Abbey.

Starring: Edwards, Elizabeths, Henrys, Annes, Marys, and poets.

Westminster Abbey Tour

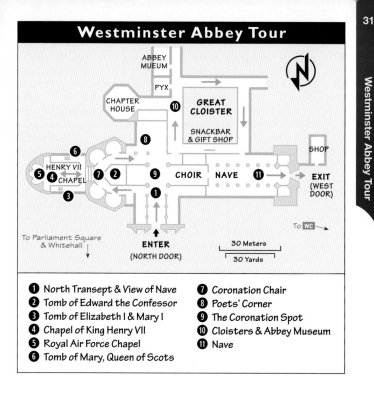

ABBEY MUSEUM

PYX

CHAPTER HOUSE

GREAT CLOISTER

SNACKBAR & GIFT SHOP

HENRY VII CHAPEL

CHOIR   NAVE

SHOP

EXIT (WEST DOOR)

To Parliament Square & Whitehall

To WC

ENTER (NORTH DOOR)

30 Meters
30 Yards

1 North Transept & View of Nave
2 Tomb of Edward the Confessor
3 Tomb of Elizabeth I & Mary I
4 Chapel of King Henry VII
5 Royal Air Force Chapel
6 Tomb of Mary, Queen of Scots
7 Coronation Chair
8 Poets' Corner
9 The Coronation Spot
10 Cloisters & Abbey Museum
11 Nave

THE TOUR BEGINS

You'll have no choice but to follow the steady flow of tourists through the church, following the route laid out by the audioguide. It's all one-way, and most days the crowds can be a real crush. Here are the Abbey's top 10 (plus one) stops.

▶ *Walk straight in, entering the north transept. Pick up the map flier that locates the most illustrious tombs, and borrow the included audioguide. Follow the crowd flow to the right, passing through* **"Scientists' Corner,"** *with memorials to Isaac Newton, Michael Faraday, Charles Darwin, and others. Enter the spacious nave.*

❶ North Transept and View of the Nave

Look down the long, narrow, high-ceilinged nave. Lined with the praying hands of the Gothic arches, glowing with light from the stained glass, it's clear that this is more than a museum. With saints in stained glass, heroes in carved stone, and the bodies of England's greatest citizens under the floor stones, Westminster Abbey is the religious heart of England.

Nestled in the nave is the enclosed area called the choir (or "quire"). In these elaborately carved wooden seats, the Abbey's original monks once chanted their services. Today, it's where the Abbey boys' choir sings the evensong. In the center of the cross-shaped church is the main altar. This altar (with cross and candlesticks), sits atop a platform, up five stairs. (More on this important spot later in the tour.)

The Abbey was built in 1065. Its name, Westminster, means Church in the West (west of St. Paul's Cathedral). For the next 250 years, the Abbey was made over and remodeled to become essentially the church you see today. An extensive 19th-century remodel preserved the original Gothic style.

The Abbey's 10-story nave is the tallest in England. The chandeliers, 10 feet tall, look small in comparison (16 were given to the Abbey by the Guinness family).

▶ *After checking out the nave, the choir, and the altar, continue on. From the altar, veer left and follow the crowd. You'll walk past the statue of Robert ("Bob") Peel, the prime minister whose policemen were nicknamed "bobbies." Stroll a few yards into the land of dead kings and queens. Use the audioguide to explore the side chapels—the Chapel of St. John the Baptist and the Chapel of St. Michael. There you'll see effigies of the dead lying atop their tombs of polished stone. They lie on*

Many dead monarchs lie admiring the Gothic ceiling.

Elizabeth I, buried alongside her sister and rival

their backs or reclining on their sides. Dressed in ruffed collars, they relax on pillows, clasping their hands in prayer, many buried side by side with their spouse.

After exploring the chapels, pause at the wooden staircase on your right.

❷ Tomb of Edward the Confessor

The holiest part of the church is the raised area behind the altar (where the wooden staircase leads—sorry, no tourist access except with verger tour). Step back and peek over the dark coffin of Edward I to see the tippy-top of the green-and-gold wedding-cake tomb of King Edward the Confessor—the man who built Westminster Abbey. It was finished just in time to bury Edward and to crown his foreign successor, William the Conqueror, in 1066.

▶ *Continue on. At the top of the stone staircase, veer left into the private burial chapel of Queen Elizabeth I.*

❸ Tomb of Queen Elizabeth I and Mary I

Although there's only one effigy on the tomb (Elizabeth's), there are actually two queens buried beneath it, both daughters of Henry VIII (by different mothers). Bloody Mary—meek, pious, sickly, and Catholic—enforced Catholicism during her short reign (1553–1558) by burning "heretics" at the stake.

Elizabeth—strong, clever, and Protestant—steered England on an Anglican course. She holds a royal orb symbolizing that she's queen of the whole globe. When 26-year-old Elizabeth was crowned in the Abbey, her right to rule was questioned because she was the bastard seed of Henry VIII's unsanctioned marriage to Anne Boleyn. But Elizabeth's long reign (1559–1603) was one of the greatest in English history, a time when England ruled the seas and Shakespeare explored human emotions. When she died, thousands poured into the Abbey for her funeral. The effigy's face, modeled after Elizabeth's death mask, is considered a very accurate take on this hook-nosed, imperious "Virgin Queen."

The two half-sisters disliked each other in life—Mary even had Elizabeth locked up in the Tower of London for a short time. Now they lie side by side for eternity. The Latin inscription ends, "Here we lie, two sisters in hope of one resurrection."

▸ *Continue into the ornate, flag-draped room behind the main altar.*

❹ Chapel of King Henry VII (a.k.a. the Lady Chapel)

The light from the stained-glass windows; the colorful banners overhead; and the elaborate tracery in stone, wood, and glass give this room the festive air of a medieval tournament. The prestigious Knights of the Bath meet here, under the magnificent ceiling studded with gold pendants. The ceiling (1519)—of carved stone, not plaster—is a textbook example of English Perpendicular Gothic and fan vaulting. The ceiling was sculpted on the floor in pieces, then jigsaw-puzzled into place.

The knights sit in the wooden stalls with their coats of arms on the back, churches on their heads, their banner flying above, and the graves of dozens of kings beneath their feet. When the Queen worships here, she sits in the southwest corner chair under the carved wooden throne with the lion crown.

Behind the small altar is an iron cage housing the tombs of Henry VII of Lancaster and Elizabeth of York, whose marriage finally settled the Wars of the Roses between those two clans. Henry and Elizabeth were the parents of Henry VIII and grandparents of Elizabeth I. This exuberant chapel heralds a new optimistic, postwar era as England prepares to step onto the world stage.

▸ *At the far end of the chapel is a modern set of stained-glass windows.*

❺ Royal Air Force Chapel

Saints in robes and halos mingle with pilots in parachutes and bomber jackets. This tribute to WWII flyers is for those who earned their angel wings in the Battle of Britain (July–Oct 1940). When Hitler's air force threatened to snuff Britain out without a fight, British pilots stepped up. These

Chapel of King Henry VII—exuberant Gothic   Coronation chair with slot for Stone of Scone

were the fighters about whom Churchill said, "Never...was so much owed by so many to so few."

The Abbey survived the Battle and the Blitz, but this window did not, so it was replaced with this modern memorial. The book of remembrances lists each of the 1,497 airmen (including one American) who died in the Battle of Britain.

▶ *Exit the Chapel of Henry VII. Turn left into a side chapel with the tomb (the central one of three in the chapel).*

❻ Tomb of Mary, Queen of Scots

Historians get dewy-eyed over the fate of Mary, Queen of Scots (1542–1587). The beautiful, French-educated queen was executed for treason by her cousin, Queen Elizabeth I. After Elizabeth —the "Virgin Queen"—died heirless, Mary's son James I became king of England. He honored his mum with the Abbey's most sumptuous tomb.

▶ *Exit Mary's chapel. Ahead of you is the Coronation Chair. (By the time you visit, the Chair may have moved to its new permanent home—in the nave, near the end of the tourist route.)*

❼ Coronation Chair

The gold-painted oak chair sits empty until the next coronation. For every English coronation since 1308 (except two), it's been moved to its spot before the high altar to receive the royal buttocks. At coronation time, the empty space below the chair holds the Stone of Scone (pronounced "skoon"), symbolizing Scotland's unity with England's monarch. It rests in its home Scotland until it's needed.

▶ *Continue on. Turn left into the south transept. You're in Poets' Corner.*

❽ Poets' Corner

England's greatest artistic contributions are in the written word. Here lie buried the masters of arguably the world's most complex and expressive language. (Many writers are honored with plaques and monuments; relatively few are actually buried here.)

▸ *Start with Chaucer, buried in the wall under the blue windows, marked with a white plaque reading* Qui Fuit Anglorum...

Geoffrey Chaucer (c. 1343–1400) is often considered the father of English literature. Chaucer's *Canterbury Tales* told of earthy people speaking everyday English. He was the first great writer buried in the Abbey (thanks to his job as a Westminster clerk). Later, it became a tradition to bury other writers here, and Poets' Corner was built around his tomb. The blue windows have blank panels awaiting the names of future poets.

▸ *The plaques on the floor before Chaucer are gravestones and memorials to many literary greats, including...*

Lord Byron, the great lover of women and adventure: "Though the night was made for loving,/And the day returns too soon,/Yet we'll go no more a-roving/By the light of the moon."

Dylan Thomas, alcoholic master of modernism, with a Romantic's heart: "Do not go gentle into that good night. Rage, rage against the dying of the light."

Alfred, Lord Tennyson, conscience of the Victorian era: "'Tis better to have loved and lost/Than never to have loved at all."

Robert Browning: "Oh, to be in England/Now that April's there."

▸ *Farther out in the south transept, you'll find a statue of...*

William Shakespeare: Although he's not buried here, this greatest of English writers is honored by a fine statue that stands near the end of the transept, overlooking the others: "Life's but a walking shadow, a poor player that struts and frets his hour upon the stage and then is heard no more."

George Frideric Handel: High on the wall opposite Shakespeare is the German immigrant famous for composing the *Messiah* oratorio: "Hallelujah, hallelujah, hallelujah." His actual tomb is on the floor, next to...

Charles Dickens, whose serialized novels brought literature to the masses: "It was the best of times, it was the worst of times."

And finally, near the center of the transept, find the small, white floor plaque of **Thomas Parr** (marked "THO: PARR"). Check the dates of his life (1483–1635) and do the math. In his (reputed) 152 years, he served 10 sovereigns and was a contemporary of Columbus, Henry VIII, Elizabeth I, Shakespeare, and Galileo.

▶ *Walk to the center of the church in front of the high altar.*

❾ The Coronation Spot

Here is where every English coronation since 1066 has taken place. Imagine the day when Prince William becomes king:

The nobles in robes and powdered wigs look on from the carved wooden stalls of the choir. The Archbishop of Canterbury stands at the high altar (table with candlesticks, up five steps). The coronation chair is placed before the altar on the round, brown pavement stone, representing the earth. Surrounding the whole area are temporary bleachers for 8,000 VIPs, going halfway up the rose windows of each transept, creating a "theater."

Long silver trumpets hung with banners sound a fanfare as the monarch-to-be enters the church. The congregation sings, "I will go into the house of the Lord," as William parades slowly down the nave and up the steps to the altar. After a church service, he sits in the chair, facing the altar, where the crown jewels are placed. William is anointed with holy oil, then receives a ceremonial sword, ring, and cup. The royal scepter is placed in his hands, and—dut, dutta dah—the archbishop lowers the Crown of St. Edward the Confessor onto his royal head. Finally, King William stands up, descends the steps, and is presented to the people. As cannons roar throughout the city, the people cry, "God save the king!"

Royalty are also given funerals here. Princess Diana's coffin lay here before her funeral service. She was then buried on her family estate. The "Queen Mum" (mother of Elizabeth II) had her funeral here. This is also often the site of royal weddings, such as the nuptials of Prince Andrew and Sarah Ferguson or Prince William and Kate Middleton.

▶ *Exit the church (temporarily) at the south door, which leads to the...*

❿ Cloisters and Abbey Museum

The buildings that adjoin the church once housed monks. (The church is known as the "abbey" because it was the headquarters of the Benedictine Order until Henry VIII kicked them out in 1540.) Cloistered courtyards gave them a place to meditate on God's creations. The cloisters also have fine views of the flying buttresses that support the church walls, which allowed Gothic architects to build so high.

The cloisters—covered walkways for monks   Memorials in the nave of great Britons

At the small Abbey Museum you can look into the impressively re-alistic eyes of Elizabeth I, Charles II, Admiral Nelson, and a dozen other wax-and-wood statues that graced coffins during funeral processions. Beyond the Abbey Museum, passageways lead to the Little Cloister and picturesque College Garden (open Tue-Thu).

▶ *Go back into the church for the last stop.*

⓫ Nave

On the floor near the west entrance of the Abbey is the flower-lined Tomb of the Unknown Warrior, one ordinary WWI soldier buried in soil from France with lettering made from melted-down weapons from that war. Think about that million-man army from the empire and commonwealth that perished in the war. Hanging on a column next to the tomb is the US Congressional Medal of Honor, presented by General Pershing in 1921 to honor England's WWI dead. Closer to the door is a memorial to the hero of World War II, Winston Churchill.

To the left of the choir screen is so-called "Scientists' Corner," with memorials to Isaac Newton, Michael Faraday, Charles Darwin, and others.

On that side of the nave, find the stained-glass window of St. Edward the Confessor (third bay from the end, marked *S: Edwardus rex...*), with crown, scepter, and ring. Thank him for the Abbey.

Finally, grab a seat in the center and look down the nave. Listen to and ponder this place, filled with the remains of the people who made Britain a world power—saints, royalty, poets, musicians, scientists, sol-diers, politicians. Now step back outside into a city filled with modern-day poets, saints, and heroes who continue to make Britain great.

National Gallery Tour

The National Gallery lets you tour Europe's art without ever crossing the Channel. Britain's best collection of paintings features all the biggies: Leonardo da Vinci, Rembrandt, Monet, Van Gogh, and more. With so many exciting artists and styles, it's a fine overture to art if you're just starting a European trip, and a pleasant reprise if you're just finishing. The "National Gal" is always a welcome interlude from the bustle of London sightseeing.

In this 90-minute sweep through Britain's best collection of paintings, we'll travel chronologically through art history: from medieval madonnas to Renaissance goddesses, from intricate Dutch detail to Baroque bombast, from British restraint to the breezy French Impressionism that leads to the modern world. We'll cruise like an eagle with wide eyes for the big picture, seeing how each style progresses into the next.

MEDIEVAL &
EARLY RENAISSANCE
1 ANONYMOUS – The Wilton Diptych
2 UCCELLO – Battle of San Romano
3 VAN EYCK – The Arnolfini Marriage

ITALIAN RENAISSANCE
4 BOTTICELLI – Venus and Mars
5 CRIVELLI – The Annunciation, with Saint Emidius

HIGH RENAISSANCE
6 MICHELANGELO – Entombment
7 RAPHAEL – Pope Julius II
8 HOLBEIN – The Ambassadors
9 DA VINCI – The Virgin of the Rocks; Virgin and Child with St. Anne and St. John the Baptist

VENETIAN RENAISSANCE
10 TINTORETTO – The Origin of the Milky Way
11 TITIAN – Bacchus and Ariadne

NORTHERN PROTESTANT ART
12 VERMEER – A Young Woman Standing at a Virginal
13 "A Peepshow"
14 REMBRANDT – Belshazzar's Feast
15 REMBRANDT – Self-Portrait

BAROQUE & ROCOCO
16 RUBENS – The Judgment of Paris
17 VAN DYCK – Equestrian Portrait of Charles I
18 VELÁZQUEZ – The Rokeby Venus
19 CARAVAGGIO –The Supper at Emmaus
20 BOUCHER – Pan and Syrinx

SAINSBURY WING
ENTRANCE ON LEVEL 0

SELF-GUIDED TOUR STARTS ON LEVEL 2

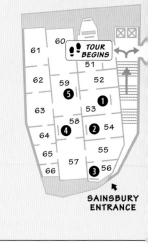

BRITISH
21 CONSTABLE – The Hay Wain
22 TURNER – The Fighting Téméraire
23 DELAROCHE – The Execution of Lady Jane Grey

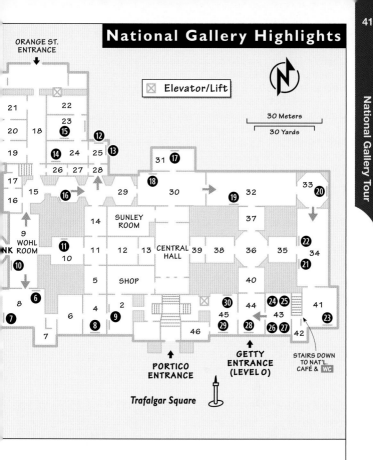

National Gallery Highlights

☒ Elevator/Lift

30 Meters
30 Yards

ORANGE ST. ENTRANCE

21 22
20 18 23 ⑮
19 ⑭ 24 ⑫ ⑬ 25
  26 27 28
17 15 ⑯ 29 ⑱ 30 → ⑲ 32 33 ⑳
16
9 14 SUNLEY ROOM 37
WOHL ROOM ⑪ 11 12 13 CENTRAL HALL 39 38 36 35 34 ㉒
NK 10 5 SHOP 40 ㉑
⑩
8 ⑥ 4 2 ㉚ 44 ㉔㉕ 41
⑦ 6 ⑧ ⑨ 45 43 ㉓
7 46 ㉙ ㉘ ㉖㉗ 42

31 ⑰ ㉚

PORTICO ENTRANCE

GETTY ENTRANCE (LEVEL 0)

STAIRS DOWN TO NAT'L. CAFÉ & WC

Trafalgar Square

IMPRESSIONISM & BEYOND
㉔ MONET – Gare St. Lazare
㉕ MONET – The Water-Lily Pond
㉖ MANET – Corner of a Café-Concert (a.k.a. The Waitress)
㉗ RENOIR – Boating on the Seine
㉘ SEURAT – Bathers at Asnières
㉙ VAN GOGH – Sunflowers
㉚ CÉZANNE – Bathers

ORIENTATION

Cost: Free, but suggested donation of £2–3. Temporary (optional) exhibits require an admission fee.

Hours: Daily 10:00–18:00, Fri until 21:00, last entry to special exhibits 45 minutes before closing.

Getting There: It's central as can be, overlooking Trafalgar Square (Tube: Charing Cross or Leicester Square).

Information: Tel. 020/7747-2885, switchboard tel. 020/7839-3321, www.nationalgallery.org.uk.

Tours: Free one-hour tours leave from the Sainsbury Entrance daily at 11:30 and 14:30, plus Fri at 19:00. The excellent £3.50 audioguide offers an array of tours plus dial-up info on any painting. The ArtStart computer terminals help you study any artist, style, or topic.

Cloakroom: Free, but £1–2 suggested donation; required only for large bags.

Photography: Photos are strictly forbidden.

Cuisine Art: There are three eateries in the Gallery. The National Dining Rooms—located on the first floor of the Sainsbury Wing—are cool, classy, and pricey for a sit-down meal (£15–20 entrées, £17 afternoon tea). The National Café—located near the Getty Entrance—has a table-service restaurant (£15–20 entrées, £15 afternoon tea) and an easier-on-the-budget sandwich/soup/salad/pastry buffet (£3–4). The Espresso Bar, also near the Getty Entrance, has soft couches, sandwiches, and ArtStart computers. Outside the Gallery, there are several options near Trafalgar Square (✪ see page 196).

Wilton Diptych—scrawny medieval figures

Uccello creates a 3-D grid

THE TOUR BEGINS

The Gallery has three entrances facing Trafalgar Square. Our tour starts from the Sainsbury Entrance, located far to the left of the central dome. The paintings are all on one floor. To see the art in chronological order requires a bit of map-reading and navigating, but it's worth it.

▸ *Enter through the Sainsbury Entrance. Pick up the handy map (£1) and climb the stairs. At the top, turn left, then left again, entering Room 52.*

Medieval and Early Renaissance (1260–1440)

In Rooms 52 and 53, you see shiny gold paintings of saints, angels, Madonnas, and crucifixions floating in an ethereal gold never-never land. One thing is very clear: Medieval heaven was different from medieval earth. The holy wore gold plates on their heads. Faces were serene and generic. People posed stiffly, facing directly out or to the side, never in between. Saints are recognized by the symbols they carry (a key, a sword, a book), rather than by their human features.

Art in the Middle Ages was religious, dominated by the Church. The illiterate faithful could meditate on an altarpiece and visualize heaven. It's as though they couldn't imagine saints and angels inhabiting the dreary world of rocks, trees, and sky we live in.

▸ *One of the finest medieval altarpieces is in a glass case in Room 53.*

❶ Anonymous—*The Wilton Diptych* (c. 1395)

Three kings (left panel) come to adore Mary and her rosy-cheeked baby (right panel), surrounded by flame-like angels. The kings have expressive faces, and the back side shows a deer in the grass. Still, the anonymous artist is struggling with reality. The figures are flat, scrawny, and sinless. Mary's exquisite fingers hold an anatomically impossible little foot. John the Baptist (among the kings) is holding a "lamb of God" that looks more like a Chihuahua. Nice try.

▸ *Continuing into Room 54, you'll leave this gold-leaf peace and find...*

❷ Uccello—*Battle of San Romano* (c. 1450)

This colorful battle scene shows the victory of Florence over Siena—and the battle for literal realism on the canvas. It's an early Renaissance attempt at a realistic, nonreligious, three-dimensional scene.

Uccello creates the illusion of distance with a background of farmyards, receding hedges, and tiny soldiers. He actually constructs a grid of fallen lances in the foreground, then places the horses and warriors within it. Still, Uccello hasn't quite worked out the bugs—the figures in the distance are far too big, and the fallen soldier on the left isn't much larger than the fallen shield on the right.

▶ *In Room 56, you'll find...*

❸ Van Eyck—*The Arnolfini Marriage* (1434)

Called by some "The Shotgun Wedding," this painting shows a solemn, well-dressed couple taking their vows, their hands joined in the center. Like a medieval dollhouse, the tiny room is chock-full of everyday furnishings painted with exquisite detail.

Feel the texture of the fabrics, count the terrier's hairs, trace the shadows generated by the window. Each object is shown in close-up focus; the beads on the back wall are as crystal clear as the bracelets on the bride. To top it off, the round mirror on the far wall reflects the whole scene backward in miniature, showing the loving couple and a pair of mysterious visitors. Is it the concerned parents? The minister? Van Eyck himself at his easel? Or has the artist painted you, the home viewer, into the scene?

By the way, the bride may not be pregnant. The fashion of the day was to wear a pillow to look pregnant in hopes she'd soon get that way. At least, that's what they told their parents.

▶ *Return to Room 55, turn left into Room 57, then turn right into Room 58.*

The Italian Renaissance (1400–1550)

The Renaissance—or "rebirth" of the culture of ancient Greece and Rome—was a cultural boom that changed people's thinking about every aspect of life. In politics, it meant democracy. In religion, it meant a move away from Church dominance and toward the assertion of man (humanism) and a more personal faith. Science and secular learning were revived after centuries of superstition and ignorance. In architecture, it was a return to the balanced columns and domes of Greece and Rome.

In painting, the Renaissance meant realism. Artists rediscovered the beauty of nature and the human body. With pictures of beautiful people in harmonious, 3-D surroundings, they expressed the optimism and confidence of this new age.

The Arnolfini Marriage—details, details

Botticelli uses ancient Greek symbolism.

Crivelli's illusion requires no 3-D glasses.

❹ Botticelli—*Venus and Mars* (c. 1485)

Mars takes a break from war, succumbing to the delights of love (Venus), while impish satyrs play innocently with the discarded tools of death. In the early spring of the Renaissance, there was an optimistic mood in the air—the feeling that enlightened Man could end war and solve problems. Here, Venus has sapped man's medieval stiffness, and the Renaissance is coming.

▶ *Continue to Room 59.*

❺ Crivelli—*The Annunciation, with Saint Emidius* (1486)

Mary, in green, is visited by the dove of the Holy Ghost, who beams down from the distant heavens in a shaft of light. It's a melange of colorful details: the hanging rug, the peacock, the architectural minutiae that lead you way, way back, then bam!—you have a giant pickle in your face.

All this is set within Italian Renaissance 3-D. The floor tiles and building bricks recede into the distance. We're sucked right in, accelerating through the alleyway, under the arch, and off into space. The Holy Ghost spans the entire distance, connecting heavenly background with earthly foreground. Crivelli creates an Escheresque labyrinth of rooms and walkways that we want to walk through, around, and into—or is that just a male thing?

Renaissance Italians were interested in—even obsessed with—portraying 3-D space. Perhaps they focused their spiritual passion away from heaven and toward the physical world. With such restless energy, they needed lots of elbow room. Space, the final frontier.

▶ *Just two rooms ahead is Room 51, where we first entered. From Room 51, cross to the main building (the West Wing) and enter the large*

Room 9. We'll return to these big, colorful canvases—but first, turn right into Room 8.

The High Renaissance (1500)

With the "Big Three" of the High Renaissance—Leonardo, Michelangelo, and Raphael—painters had finally conquered realism. These three Florence-trained artists carefully composed their figures on the canvas, "building" them into geometrical patterns that reflected the balance and order they saw in nature.

⑥ Michelangelo—*Entombment* (unfinished, c. 1500–1501)

Michelangelo, the greatest sculptor ever, proves it here in this "painted sculpture" of the crucified Jesus being carried to the tomb. Like a chiseled Greek god, the musclehead in red ripples beneath his clothes. The men strain to hold up Christ's body, and in their tension we, too, feel the great weight and tragedy of their dead god. Christ's naked body—shocking to the medieval Church—was completely acceptable in the Renaissance world, where the classical nudes seemed to sum up all that was good in man. Michelangelo lets the bodies do the talking, expressing the divine through the human form.

Renaissance balance and symmetry reign. Christ is the center of the composition, flanked by two supporters who are, in turn, flanked by two others. The painting is unfinished, with a blank space in the lower right where Mary would have been.

⑦ Raphael—*Pope Julius II* (1511)

The worldly, Renaissance Pope Julius II—who was more a swaggering

Michelangelo's bodybuilder saints

Raphael—psychological realism

conquistador than a pious pope—set out to rebuild Rome in Renaissance style, hiring Michelangelo to paint the ceiling of the Vatican's Sistine Chapel.

Raphael gives a behind-the-scenes look at this complex man. On the one hand, the pope is an imposing pyramid of power, with a velvet shawl, silk shirt, and fancy rings boasting of wealth and success. But at the same time, he appears bent and broken, his throne backed into a corner, with an expression that seems to say, "Is this all there is?"

▶ *Exit Room 8 (opposite where you entered), and pass through Room 6 to reach Room 4.*

❽ Holbein—*The Ambassadors* (1533)

German-born Hans Holbein created this portrait for England's Renaissance Man, Henry VIII. Two well-dressed, suave men flank a shelf full of books, globes, navigational tools, and musical instruments—objects that sym-

Holbein's *Ambassadors* epitomize Renaissance worldliness.

bolize the secular knowledge of the Renaissance. Almost forgotten is the tiny crucifix in the upper-left corner.

So what's with the gray, slanting blob at the bottom? If you view the blob from the right-hand edge of the painting (get real close, right up to the frame), the blob suddenly becomes...a skull. In painting terms, the optical illusion is called an anamorphic projection. Symbolically, the skull is a *memento mori*, a reminder that—despite the fine clothes, proud poses, and worldly knowledge—we will all die.

▶ *Continue into Room 2, with two works by Leonardo.*

⑨ Leonardo da Vinci—*The Virgin of the Rocks* (1508)

Mary, the mother of Jesus, plays with her son and little Johnny the Baptist (with cross, at left) while an androgynous angel looks on. Leonardo brings this holy scene right down to earth by setting it among rocks, stalactites, water, and flowering plants. But looking closer, we see that Leonardo has deliberately posed his people into a pyramid shape, with Mary's head at the peak, creating an oasis of maternal stability and serenity amid the hard rock of the earth. Leonardo, who was illegitimate, may have sought in his art the young mother he never knew. Freud thought so.

▶ *Also in Room 2, you'll find...*

Leonardo da Vinci—*Virgin and Child with St. Anne and St. John the Baptist* (c. 1499-1500)

This chalk drawing, or cartoon, shows two children at play—oblivious to the violent deaths they'll both suffer—beneath their mothers' Mona Lisa smiles.

But follow the eyes: Shadowy-eyed Anne turns toward Mary, who

Leonardo's *Virgin*—a maternal pyramid

Leonardo's sketch—all eyes lead to Jesus

looks tenderly down to Jesus, who blesses John, who gazes back dreamily. As your eyes follow theirs, you're led back to the literal and psychological center of the composition—Jesus—the Alpha and Omega.

This sketch—pieced together from two separate papers (see the line down the middle)—gives us an inside peek at Leonardo's genius.

▶ *The Renaissance—born in Florence and nurtured in Rome—soon shifted to Venice. Backtrack to the long Room 9.*

Venetian Renaissance (1510–1600)

Venice got wealthy by trading with the luxurious and exotic East. Its happy-go-lucky art style shows a taste for the finer things in life. The canvases are bigger, the colors brighter. Chaste Madonnas and noble saints are replaced by pagan gods and sexy, golden centerfolds.

⑩ Tintoretto—*The Origin of the Milky Way* (c. 1575)

The promiscuous god Jupiter places his illegitimate son, baby Hercules, at his wife's breast. Juno says, "Wait a minute. That's not my baby!" Her milk spurts upward, becoming the Milky Way.

Tintoretto places us right up in the clouds, among the gods, who swirl around at every angle. Jupiter appears to be flying almost right at us. An X composition unites it all—Juno slants one way while Jupiter tilts the other.

▶ *Find a colorful, raucous parade in the adjoining Room 10.*

⑪ Titian—*Bacchus and Ariadne* (1523)

Bacchus, the god of wine, leaps from his leopard-drawn chariot, his red cape blowing behind him, to cheer up Ariadne (far left), who has been jilted by her lover. Bacchus' motley entourage rattles cymbals, bangs on

Tintoretto—"That's not my baby!"

Titian—Bacchus makes a raucous entrance

tambourines, and literally shakes a leg. Man and animal mingle in this pre-Christian orgy, with leopards, a snake, a dog, satyrs (part man, part goat), and butchered donkey parts ready for the barbecue.

With this painting, Titian the Venetian (see his "Ticianus" signature on the gold vase, lower left) brings Renaissance worldliness to its logical conclusion. The fat, sleepy guy in the background has had enough.

▶ *Return to Room 9 and turn right. Exit this room at the far end and turn right, entering the long Room 29 (with mint-green wallpaper). Midway through Room 29, turn left and find Room 25.*

Northern Protestant Art (1600–1700)

Big change. We switch from CinemaScope format to smaller canvases, subdued colors, everyday scenes, and not even a bare shoulder.

Money shapes art. The Northern countries' art-buyers were hard-working, middle-class, Protestant merchants. They wanted simple, cheap, no-nonsense pictures to decorate their homes and offices. Greek gods and Virgin Marys were out, hometown folks and hometown places were in—portraits, landscapes, still lifes, and slice-of-life scenes. Painted with great attention to detail, this is art meant not to wow or preach at you, but to be enjoyed and lingered over. Sightsee.

⑫ **Vermeer—***A Young Woman Standing at a Virginal* (c. 1670)
Inside a simple Dutch home, a prim virgin plays an early piano called a "virginal." We've surprised her, and she pauses to look up at us.

By framing off such a small world to look at—from the blue chair in the foreground to the wall in back—Vermeer forces us to appreciate the tiniest details, the beauty of everyday things. We can meditate on the tiles lining

Vermeer—the beauty of everyday things

Rembrandt—Belshazzar's uh-oh moment

the floor, the subtle shades of the white wall, and the pale, diffused light that seeps in from the window. The painting of a nude cupid on the back wall only strengthens this virgin's purity.

▶ *Also in Room 25, you'll find*  *"A Peepshow," an ingenious box-like device that brings a house interior to three-dimensional life. Next, enter the adjoining Room 24.*

⑭ Rembrandt—*Belshazzar's Feast* (c. 1635)

The wicked king has been feasting with God's sacred dinnerware when the meal is interrupted. Belshazzar turns to see the hand of God, burning an ominous message into the wall that Belshazzar's number is up. As he turns, he knocks over a goblet of wine. The drama is accentuated by the strong contrast between dark brown and harsh light, a Rembrandt specialty.

Rembrandt captures the scene at the most ironic moment. Belshazzar is about to be ruined. We know it, his guests know it, and, judging by the look on his face, he's coming to the same conclusion.

▶ *Enter the adjoining Room 23.*

⑮ Rembrandt—*Self-Portrait* (1669)

Rembrandt throws the light of truth on...himself. This craggy self-portrait was done the year he died, at age 63. Contrast it with one done three decades earlier (hanging directly opposite). Rembrandt, the greatest Dutch painter, started out as the successful, wealthy young genius of the art world. But he refused to crank out commercial works. Rembrandt painted things that he believed in but no one would invest in—family members, down-to-earth Bible scenes, and self-portraits like these.

Here, Rembrandt surveys the wreckage of his independent life. He

Rembrandt—proud self-portrait

Rubens—dimpled-cheek Baroque excess

was bankrupt, his mistress had just died, and he had also buried several of his children. We see a disillusioned, well-worn, but proud old genius.

▶ *Backtrack to the long, mint-green Room 29.*

Baroque (1600–1700)

⑯ Rubens

This room holds big, colorful, emotional works by Peter Paul Rubens and others from Catholic Flanders (Belgium). While Protestant and democratic Europe painted simple scenes, Catholic and aristocratic countries turned to the style called Baroque. Baroque art took what was flashy in Venetian art and made it flashier, gaudy and made it gaudier, dramatic and made it shocking.

Rubens painted anything that would raise your pulse—battles, miracles, hunts, and, especially, fleshy women with dimples on all four cheeks. For instance, *The Judgment of Paris* (one of two versions in this museum by Rubens) is little more than an excuse for a study of the female nude, showing front, back, and profile all on one canvas.

▶ *Exit Room 29 at the far end. In Room 30 (with red wallpaper), turn left into the big, red Room 31, where you'll see a large canvas.*

⑰ Van Dyck—Equestrian Portrait of Charles I (c. 1637–1638)

King Charles sits on a huge horse, accentuating his power. The horse's small head makes sure that little Charles isn't dwarfed. Charles was a soft-on-Catholics king in a hard-core Protestant country until England's Civil War (1648), when his genteel head was separated from his refined body by Cromwell and company.

King Charles I, divine monarch   Velázquez's racy *Venus*

Kings and bishops used the grandiose Baroque style to impress the masses with their power. Van Dyck's portrait style set the tone for all the stuffy, boring portraits of British aristocrats who wished to be portrayed as sophisticated gentlemen—whether they were or not.

▶ *For the complete opposite of a stuffy portrait, backpedal into Room 30 for...*

⓲ Velázquez—*The Rokeby Venus* (c. 1647-1651)

Like a Venetian centerfold, she lounges diagonally across the canvas, admiring herself, with flaring red, white, and gray fabrics to highlight her rosy-white skin and inflame our passion. Horny Spanish kings loved Titianesque nudes, despite that country's strict Inquisition. This work by the king's personal court painter is the first (and, for over a century, the only) Spanish nude. About the sole concession to Spanish modesty is the false reflection in the mirror—if it really showed what the angle should show, Velázquez would have needed two mirrors...and a new job.

▶ *Turning your left cheek to hers, tango into Room 32.*

⓳ Caravaggio—*The Supper at Emmaus* (1601)

After Jesus was crucified, he rose from the dead and appeared without warning to some of his followers. Jesus just wants a quiet meal, but the man in green, suddenly realizing who he's eating with, is about to jump out of his chair in shock.

Caravaggio exaggerated the grittiness of life, modeling his saints after real, ugly, un-haloed people. His paintings look like how a wet dog smells. From the torn shirts to the five o'clock shadows, we are witnessing a very human miracle.

▶ *Leave Room 32 at the far end, and enter Room 33.*

French Rococo (1700–1800)

As Europe's political and economic center shifted from Italy to France, Louis XIV's court at Versailles became its cultural hub. Every aristocrat spoke French, dressed French, and bought French paintings. The Rococo art of Louis' successors was as frilly, sensual, and suggestive as the decadent French court. We see their rosy-cheeked portraits and their fantasies: lords and ladies at play in classical gardens, where mortals and gods cavort together.

▶ *One of the finest examples is the tiny...*

Caravaggio—Bible stories with everyday people

Boucher—Pan seeks a threesome

🔹 Boucher—*Pan and Syrinx* (1739–1759)

Curious Pan seeks a threesome, but Syrinx eventually changes to reeds, leaving him all wet. Rococo art is like a Rubens that got shrunk in the wash—smaller, lighter pastel colors, frillier, and more delicate than the Baroque style. Same dimples, though.

▶ *Enter Room 34. Take a hike around and enjoy the English-country-garden ambience.*

British (1800–1850)

🔹 Constable—*The Hay Wain* (1821)

The more reserved British were more comfortable cavorting with nature than with the lofty gods. John Constable set up his easel out-of-doors, painstakingly capturing the simple majesty of billowing clouds, billowing trees, and everyday rural life. His rustic style was actually considered shocking in its day, scandalizing art lovers used to the highfalutin, prettified sheen of Baroque and Rococo.

🔹 Turner—*The Fighting Téméraire* (before 1839)

During the Industrial Revolution, machines began to replace humans, factories belched smoke over Constable's hay cart, and cloud-gazers had to punch the clock. Alas, here a modern steamboat symbolically drags a famous but obsolete sailing battleship off into the sunset to be destroyed.

Turner gives us our first glimpse into the world of "modern" art; his messy, colorful style influenced the Impressionists. Turner takes an ordinary scene (like Constable), captures the play of light with messy paints (like the Impressionists), and charges it with mystery (like, wow).

Constable—painted nature, not Greek gods

Delaroche—drama from the Tower of London

▶ *To view more work by Turner, Constable, and other British artists, visit London's Tate Britain. For now, enter Room 41.*

㉓ Delaroche—*The Execution of Lady Jane Grey* (1833)

It's 1554. The teenage queen's nine-day reign has reached its curfew. This innocent girl, manipulated into power politics by cunning advisors, is now sent to the execution site in the Tower of London. As her friends swoon with grief, she's blindfolded and forced to kneel at the chopping block. Legend has it that the confused, humiliated girl was left crawling around, groping for the block, crying out, "Where is it? What am I supposed to do?" The executioner in scarlet looks on with as much compassion as he can muster.

Britain's distinct contribution to art history is this Pre-Raphaelite style, showing medieval scenes in luminous realism with a mood of understated tragedy.

▶ *Exit Room 41 and enter Room 43. The Impressionist paintings are scattered throughout Rooms 43–46.*

Impressionism and Beyond (1850–1910)

For 500 years, a great artist was someone who could paint the real world with perfect accuracy. Then along came the camera and, click, the artist was replaced by a machine. But unemployed artists refused to go the way of *The Fighting Téméraire*.

They couldn't match the camera for painstaking detail, but they could match it—even beat it—in capturing color, the fleeting moment, the candid pose, the play of light and shadow, the quick impression a scene makes on you. A new breed of artists bursts out of the stuffy confines of the studio.

Seurat—lots of dots to "build" a scene

They donned scarves and berets and set up their canvases in farmers' fields or carried their notebooks into crowded cafés, dashing off quick sketches in order to catch a momentary...impression.

▶ *Start with the misty Monet train station.*

㉔ Monet—*Gare St. Lazare* (1877) and ㉕ *The Water-Lily Pond* (1899)

Claude Monet, the father of Impressionism, was more interested in the play of light off his subject than the subject itself. In Gare St. Lazare, he uses smudges of white and gray paint to capture how sun filters through the glass roof of the train station and is refiltered through the clouds of steam.

At his home at Giverny, near Paris, Monet created his own perfect landscape. He planned an artificial garden, rechanneled a stream, built a bridge, and planted water lilies. He painted these scenes time and again, but—because it was always a different day, with different sunlight, inspiring a different mood—each painting was unique.

㉖ Manet—*Corner of a Café-Concert* (a.k.a. *The Waitress*, 1878–1880), and ㉗ Renoir—*Boating on the Seine* (1879–1880)

Imagine just how mundane (and therefore shocking) these quick "impressions" of ordinary scenes must have been to a public that was raised on Greek gods, luscious nudes, and glowing Madonnas.

▶ *In Room 44, you'll find...*

㉘ Seurat—*Bathers at Asnières* (1883–1884)

Viewed from about 15 feet away, this is a bright, sunny scene of people lounging on a riverbank. Now move in close. The "scene" breaks up into almost random patches of bright colors. The "green" grass is a shag rug of green, yellow, red, brown, purple, and white brushstrokes. The boy's "red" cap is a collage of red, yellow, and blue. Up close, it looks like a mess of dots, but when you back up to a proper distance, *voilà!* It shimmers.

This kind of broken-up brushwork (where you can actually see individual brushstrokes) is one of the telltale signs of Impressionism. Seurat (a Post-Impressionist) takes the Impressionist color technique to its logical extreme.

▶ *In Room 45...*

㉙ Van Gogh—*Sunflowers* (1888)

In military terms, Van Gogh was the point man of his culture. He went ahead of his cohorts, explored the unknown, and caught a bullet young. He added emotion to Impressionism, infusing his love of life even into inanimate objects. These sunflowers, painted with characteristic swirling brushstrokes, shimmer and writhe in either agony or ecstasy—depending on your own mood.

Van Gogh painted these during his stay in southern France, a time of frenzied creativity, when he hovered between agony and ecstasy, bliss and madness. A year later, he shot himself.

In his day, Van Gogh was a penniless nobody, selling only one painting in his whole career. In 1987, a similar *Sunflowers* painting (he did a half-dozen versions) sold for $40 million (a salary of about $2,500 a day for 45 years), and that's not even his highest-priced painting. Hmm.

㉚ Cézanne—*Bathers* (*Les Grandes Baigneuses*, c. 1900–1906)

These bathers are arranged in strict triangles à la Leonardo—the five nudes on the left form one triangle, the seated nude on the right forms

Van Gogh's *Sunflowers* bloom eternally at the National Gallery.

Cézanne bridges Impressionism and Cubism.

another, and even the background trees and clouds are triangular patterns of paint.

Cézanne uses the Impressionist technique of building a figure with dabs of paint. But his "dabs" are often larger-sized "cube" shapes that inspired a radical new art style—Cubism.

We've traveled from medieval spirituality to Renaissance realism to Baroque elegance to Impressionist colors. Cézanne brings art into the 20th century. Now complete your walk through history by spilling out into the hubbub of 21st century London.

▸ *Exiting Room 45, you find yourself in the stairwell of the Gallery's main entrance (under the dome) on Trafalgar Square. If you want to return to the Sainsbury Entrance, cross the stairwell and pass through several familiar rooms (with Leonardo,* The Ambassadors, *etc.). In Room 9, turn left to reach the Sainsbury Wing. After perusing 700 years of art, consider one of the Gallery's eateries for a well-deserved break.*

West End Walk

From Leicester Square to Piccadilly Circus

The West End, the area just west of the original walled City of London, is London's liveliest neighborhood. Here is where you'll feel the pulse of the living, breathing London of today. Theaters, pubs, restaurants, bookstores, ethnic food, markets, and boutiques attract rock stars, punks, tourists, and ladies and gentlemen stepping from black cabs for a night on the town.

This three-hour walk samples the entertainment energy at Leicester Square, the festivity of Covent Garden, the rock and roll history of Denmark Street, the bohemian vibe of Soho, the shopping hustle and bustle of Carnaby and Regent Streets, and the neon hub of Piccadilly Circus.

West End Walk

Part 1
1. Leicester Square
2. Covent Garden
3. Charing Cross Road
4. Denmark Street
5. Soho Square
6. Strolling Through Soho
7. Brewer Street

Part 2
8. Carnaby Street
9. Regent Street
10. Piccadilly Circus
11. Piccadilly Street
12. Jermyn Street

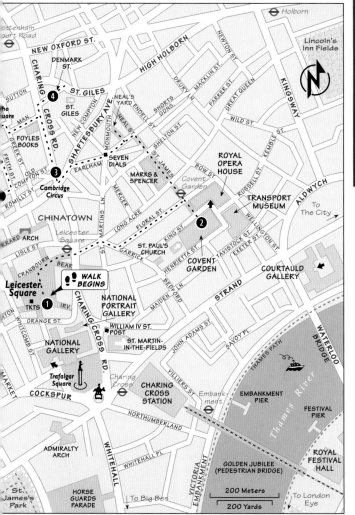

THE WALK BEGINS

Start at Leicester Square (Tube: Leicester Square). This walk is fun by day (for shopping) or by night (for nightlife). Early evenings are ideal, since most shops stay open at least until 18:00, and there's the bustle of the after-work crowd grabbing dinner or a show.

▶ *Stand at the top of Leicester Square and take in the scene.*

❶ Leicester Square

Leicester (LESS-ter) Square is ground zero for London entertainment. It's ringed with the city's glitziest **cinemas**—the Odeon (Britain's largest cinema), Empire, and Vue—all famous for hosting red-carpet movie premieres. When Tom Cruise, Angelina Jolie, or Brad Pitt need a publicity splash, it'll likely be here. (Google "London film premieres" to find upcoming events.) On any given night, this entire area is a mosh-pit of club-goers and partying teens in town from the suburbs.

The Square is the central clearinghouse for theater ticket sales. Check out the **tkts kiosk** and ignore all the other establishments that bill themselves as "half-price" but are just normal booking agencies. It's usually cheaper still to buy tickets directly from one of the theatres we'll pass on this walk.

Capital Radio London (next to the Odeon) plays a role in British rock and roll history. Back in the 1960s, the BBC was the only radio station in town, and it was mostly talk and Bach, with a smattering of pop. The British Invasion was in full swing—the Beatles, the Stones, The Who—but Brits couldn't hear it! They had to resort to "pirate" radio stations, beamed from Luxembourg or from ships at sea. Finally in 1973, Capital Radio was

Leicester Square's cinemas host red-carpet premieres.

Rock and roll history in London

Covent Garden—people-watching

Covent Garden—browsing the shops

allowed to play rock music. Today, FM 95.8 carries on as a major Top-40 broadcasting power.

▶ *Exit Leicester Square from its top corner, heading east (past the Vue cinema) on Cranbourn Street. Cross Charing Cross Road and continue along Cranbourn to the six-way intersection, then angle right onto Garrick Street. Shortly afterward, turn left onto calm, brick-lined Floral Street, with its tidy assortment of fashion boutiques. At James Street, turn right and head for...*

❷ Covent Garden

Covent Garden (only tourists pluralize the name) is a large square teeming with people and street performers—jugglers, sword swallowers, and guitar players. London's buskers (including those in the Tube) are auditioned, licensed, and assigned times and places where they are allowed to perform.

The square's centerpiece is an iron-and-glass covered marketplace. A market has been here since medieval times, when it was the "convent" garden owned by Westminster Abbey. Covent Garden remained a produce market until 1973, when its venerable arcades were converted to boutiques, cafés, and antiques shops. Besides the shops inside, a less formal market scene still thrives around the fringes.

Pan the square to find the world-class **Royal Opera House** (with a low-profile entrance in the northeast corner of the square) and the **London Transport Museum** (southeast corner). **St. Paul's Church** (not the famous cathedral) is to the west, with its Greek temple–like facade and blue clock face. St. Paul's is known as the Actors' Church, and its interior is lined with memorials to theater folk, some of whom (Chaplin, Karloff) you might recognize. The church is still a favorite of nervous performers praying for success.

▶ *Now browse your way northwest, along some lively and colorful streets.*

❸ From Covent Garden to Charing Cross Road

First backtrack two blocks up James Street, jog right, then continue straight (along the side of Marks & Spencer) up narrow Neal Street. Turn left on Short's Gardens, and find the tight alley (on the right) leading to the cozy, funky courtyard called Neal's Yard, with a thriving veggie restaurant scene. Back on Short's Gardens, Neal's Yard Dairy (at #17) sells a wide variety of artisanal cheeses from the British Isles, and gives out samples if you ask nicely.

Continue along Short's Gardens to the next intersection—called **Seven Dials**—where seven sundials atop a pole mark the meeting of seven small streets. Continue more or less straight ahead onto Earlham Street.

Bearing left, you'll spill out into **Cambridge Circus**—the busy intersection of Shaftesbury Avenue and Charing Cross Road—with its fine red-brick Victorian architecture and classic theaters. Charing Cross Road is the traditional home of London's bookstores.

▶ *Turn right (north) up Charing Cross Road. You'll pass one of the biggest bookstores, Foyles Books, which often hosts free book signings and jazz music (usually around 18:00, at 113 Charing Cross Road, www.foyles.co.uk).*

Continue a few steps north on Charing Cross, and turn right onto Denmark Street.

Seven Dials intersection

Denmark Street—home of British rock and roll

❹ Denmark Street

This seemingly nondescript little street is a musician's mecca. In the 1920s, it was known as "Britain's Tin Pan Alley"—the center of the UK's music-publishing industry, when songwriters here cranked out popular tunes printed as sheet music.

Later, in the 1960s, Denmark Street was the epicenter of rock and roll's British Invasion, which brought so much great pop music to the US. **Regent Sounds Studio** (at #4, on the right) was a low-budget recording studio. It was one of several studios on the street that recorded the Rolling Stones ("Not Fade Away"), the Kinks (who wrote a song called "Denmark Street"), the Beatles ("Fixing a Hole"), and the Who ("I Can See for Miles"). Today, Regent is a music store.

The storefront at #20 (on the left, now Wunjo Guitars) was former-ly a music publishing house, which employed a lowly office boy named Reginald Dwight. In 1969, on the building's rooftop, he wrote "Your Song," and went on to become famous as Elton John. In the 1970s, the Sex Pistols lived in apartments above #6 (on the right). The 12 Bar Café (at #25, on the left) features live music, and helped launch the careers of more recent acts: Damien Rice, KT Tunstall, Jeff Buckley, and Keane.

Today, Denmark Street offers one-stop shopping for the mod-ern musician. Without leaving this short street, you could buy a vintage Rickenbacker guitar, get your sax repaired, take piano lessons, lay down a bass track, have a few beers, or tattoo your name across your fist like Ozzy Osbourne. Notice the bulletin board in the alley alongside the 12 Bar Café (through the doorway marked #27). If you're a musician looking for a band to play in, this could be your connection.

▶ *From Denmark Street, go back across Charing Cross Road and head down Manette Street (alongside Foyles). Pass by the Borderline night-club (down the lane called Orange Yard), where R.E.M. and Oasis have played. Continue down Manette Street and under the passage, then turn right up Greek Street to...*

❺ Soho Square

The Soho neighborhood is London's version of New York City's Greenwich Village. It's ritzy, raffish, edgy, and colorful. Having escaped modern urban development, it retains a quiet, residential, pedestrian-friendly feel.

Soho Square Gardens is a favorite place on a sunny afternoon. The little house in the middle of the square is the gardener's hut. At #1, on

Chinatown's entrance

the west (left) side of the square, the MPL building (McCartney Publishing Limited) houses offices of the 120th richest man in Britain, Sir Paul McCartney.

▶ *At the bottom of the square, wander down Frith Street.*

❻ Strolling Through Soho

The restaurants and boutiques here and on adjoining streets (e.g., Greek, Dean, and Wardour Streets) are trendy and creative, the kind that attract high society when they feel like slumming it. Bars with burly, well-dressed bouncers abound.

Ronnie Scott's Jazz Club (#47 Frith Street) has featured big-name acts for 50 years. In 1970, Jimi Hendrix jammed here with Eric Burdon and War in the last performance before his death, a few days later, in a London apartment.

Turn right on Old Compton Street. You're at the center of the neighborhood (and London's gay scene), surrounded by the buzz of Soho. Take in the eclectic variety of people going by.

At the corner of Old Compton and Dean Street, look south on Dean Street. The pagoda-style arch in the distance marks London's underwhelming Chinatown, with Gerrard Street as its spine.

▶ *Continue along Old Compton Street to where it squeezes down into a narrow alley (Tisbury Court). Penetrate this sleazy passage of sex shows and blue-video shops, tolerate the barkers' raunchy come-ons, then jog a half-block right and turn left on Brewer Street.*

❼ Brewer Street: Sleaze, Porn Shops, and Prostitutes

Soho was a bordello zone in the 19th century. A bit of that survives today in this area. Sex shops, video arcades, and prostitution mingle with upscale restaurants here in west Soho. While it's illegal in Britain to sell sex on the street, well-advertised "models" entertain (profitably) in their tiny apartments. Berwick Street hosts a daily produce market.

▶ *When you reach the intersection of Brewer Street and Sherwood Street (which is also called Lower James Street), turn right and walk two blocks north (on what is now called Upper James Street). Then jog left at Beak Street to find...*

❽ Carnaby Street

In the Swinging '60s, when Pete Townsend needed a paisley shirt, John Lennon a Nehru jacket, or Twiggy a miniskirt, they came here—where those mod fashions were invented. Today, there's not a hint of hippie. For the most part, Carnaby Street looks like everything else from the '60s does now—sanitized and co-opted by upscale franchises. At least the upper end of the street retains a whiff of funkiness.

▶ *Walk north, the length of Carnaby Street, turn left on Great Marlborough Street, and head to Regent Street. You'll pass the venerable Liberty department store in the faux-Tudor building, known for its "Liberty Print" patterned cloth. At Regent Street, begin strolling downhill.*

❾ The Shops of Regent Street

You're in the heart of London's high-class, top-dollar shopping neighborhood. Regent Street has wide sidewalks and fine architecture, and most of the shops call the Queen their landlord, as she owns much of the land.

Regent Street bends with the latest fashion trends.

Just downhill from Liberty, follow the giddy kids to **Hamleys** (at #188–196), Britain's biggest toy store. In 2010 it marked its 250th anniversary of delighting children. Seven floors buzz with 28,000 toys, managed by a staff of 200. Employees, some dressed in playful costumes, give demos of the latest gadgets.

Continuing along the street, you'll pass fine bits of old English class. **Burberry** (on the right, at #167) was once dowdy—the Queen's choice—but now hip. **Hackett** (right, at #143–147) is the place to go for preppy young English menswear. **Mappin and Webb** (left, at #132) is the queen's jeweler. **Penhaligon's** (right, at #125) is the quintessential English perfumery, where royals shop for classic English scents like lavender and rose.

▶ *Regent Street arcs seductively into the ever-vibrant...*

❿ Piccadilly Circus

London's most touristy square got its name from the fancy ruffled shirts—*picadils*—made in the neighborhood long ago. This once-stately square has now (believe it or not) become home to gimmicky businesses like the gargantuan Ripley's Believe-It-Or-Not Museum. Kitschy stores like **Lillywhites** and **Cool Brittania** dispense English soccer jerseys and Union Jack underwear. At night, when neon pulses, the 20-foot-high Coke ads paint the classic Georgian facades pink. Until just a couple of years ago, this was a famously busy traffic circle, with cars and big red buses spinning around the tipsy-but-perfectly-balanced Eros statue in the center. Now it's a packed people zone. Black cabs honk, tourists crowd the attractions, and Piccadilly shows off big-city London at its glitziest.

▶ *From Piccadilly Circus, turn right and wander down the busy...*

⓫ Piccadilly Street

Escape from the frenzy of Piccadilly Street into quiet **Waterstone's** (at #203), Europe's largest bookshop, with a hip fifth floor bar with great views. Pass Christopher Wren's **St. James's Church** and you'll reach the **Fortnum & Mason** department store (#181), which feels classier and more relaxed than Harrods. At the top of the hour, the fancy clock on the facade chimes and the venerable store's founders—Fortnum and Mason—come out and bow to each other.

Consider capping this walk with a traditional afternoon tea. My two favorite places are nearby: **Fortnum & Mason** (with several restaurants and price ranges) and **The Wolseley** (a block farther west at #160 Piccadilly Street).

▶ *But first, continue a half-block west on Piccadilly Street, then turn left down the Piccadilly Arcade, which leads to quiet...*

Piccadilly—Eros statue and glitzy ads

Afternoon "tea" can be a small meal.

Beau Brummel statue amid Jermyn Street shops

⑫ Jermyn Street

A statue of Beau Brummell, the ultimate dandy, meets you as if to say, "Peruse the neighborhood's numerous fine gentleman's shirtmakers and many other delightful shops." It was Brummell (1778–1840) who popularized the understated jacket-trousers-and-tie ensemble that men still wear today. As the quote on his statue reads, "To be truly elegant, one should not be noticed."

Bates Hats (#73 Jermyn Street) still sells bowlers and top hats, as it has for a century. **Turnbull & Asser** (#71) has dressed Winston Churchill, Prince Charles, and James Bond with its "bespoke" (custom-made) shirts and suits. **Tricker's** (#67) has been making shoes for the gentleman since the days of Beau Brummell.

▸ *Our walk is finished. Consider an elegant tea nearby, shop for an elegant ascot, or head back to Piccadilly Square and pick up some Union Jack underwear.*

British Museum Tour

In the 19th century, the British flag flew over one-fourth of the world, and England collected art as fast as it collected colonies. The British Museum became *the* chronicle of Western civilization. It's the only place I can think of where you can follow the rise and fall of three great cultures in a few hours with a coffee break in the middle.

See pharaohs and their mummies from ancient Egypt, and the multi-lingual Rosetta Stone. From mighty Assyria come truck-sized statues and poignant scenes of hunted lions. The finale is the Elgin Marbles, the renowned sculptures that once decorated the Parthenon of Golden Age Greece. While the sun never set on the British Empire, it will set on you, so on this tour we'll see just the most exciting two hours.

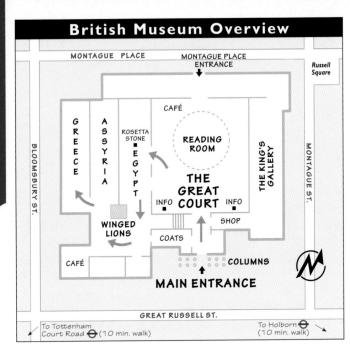

British Museum Overview

MONTAGUE PLACE

MONTAGUE PLACE ENTRANCE

Russell Square

CAFÉ

GREECE

ASSYRIA

ROSETTA STONE

EGYPT

READING ROOM

THE KING'S GALLERY

THE GREAT COURT

INFO

INFO

WINGED LIONS

COATS

SHOP

CAFÉ

COLUMNS

MAIN ENTRANCE

BLOOMSBURY ST.

MONTAGUE ST.

GREAT RUSSELL ST.

To Tottenham Court Road (10 min. walk)

To Holborn (10 min. walk)

ORIENTATION

Cost: Free, but a £5 donation is requested. Interesting temporary exhibits often require a separate (optional) admission.

Hours: Open daily 10:00–17:30, Fri until 20:30 (most galleries).

Avoiding Crowds: Rainy days and Sundays are most crowded; weekday late afternoons are least crowded.

Getting There: The main entrance is on Great Russell Street. From the Tottenham Court Road Tube station, take exit #3, turn right, and follow the brown signs four blocks to the museum. The Holborn and Russell Square Tube stops are also nearby.

Information: General info tel. 020/7323-8299. For questions on the collection, call 020/7323-8838. www.britishmuseum.org.

Entrance to the British Museum

Tours: The free 30-minute eyeOpener tours focus on select rooms (offered about every 15 minutes). The £5 audio/multimedia guide offers dial-up information on 200 objects, as well as several theme tours. A free Rick Steves audio tour of the British Museum is available on iTunes, Google Play, or at www.ricksteves.com.

Cloakroom: £1.50 per item. Large backpacks must be checked.

Photography: Photos allowed without flash or tripod (but prohibited in the temporary exhibits).

Cuisine Art: In the Great Court entrance lobby, there's the self-service Court Café on ground level (£4–5 sandwiches and salads) and the pricier Court Restaurant up the stairs (£15–20 entrees). The cafeteria-style Gallery Café (£8 hot dishes) is deeper into the museum, near the Greek art in Room 12. Near the museum, there are lots of fast, cheap, and colorful eateries along Great Russell Street.

THE TOUR BEGINS

The main entrance on Great Russell Street spills you into the Great Court, a glass-domed space with the round Reading Room in the center. (The Reading Room is impressive to visit, but not always open to visitors.) From the Great Court, doorways lead to all wings. To the left—in the West Wing—are the exhibits on Egypt, Assyria, and Greece—our tour.

▶ *Enter the Egyptian Gallery. The Rosetta Stone is directly in front of you.*

Egypt (3000 B.C.– A.D. 1)

Egypt was one of the world's first "civilizations"—that is, a group of people with a government, religion, art, a written language, and the free time to appreciate them. The Egypt we think of—pyramids, mummies, pharaohs, and guys who walk funny—lasted from 3000 to 1000 B.C. with hardly any change in the government, religion, or arts. Imagine two millennia of Eisenhower.

① The Rosetta Stone (196 B.C.)

When this rock was unearthed in the Egyptian desert in 1799, it was a sensation in Europe. This black slab caused a quantum leap in the evolution of history. Finally, Egyptian writing could be decoded.

The writing in the upper part of the stone is known as hieroglyphics, indecipherable for a thousand years. Did a picture of a bird mean "bird"? Or was it a sound, forming part of a larger word, like "burden"? As it turned out, hieroglyphics are a complex combination of the two, surprisingly more phonetic than symbolic. (For example, the hieroglyph that looks like a mouth or eye is the letter "R.")

Rosetta Stone—inscribed in three languages

Ramesses

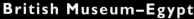

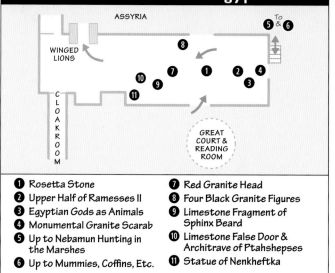

British Museum–Egypt

ASSYRIA

To **5** & **6**

WINGED
LIONS

8

10 **9** **7** **1** **2** **4**
3

11

C
L
O
A
K
R
O
O
M

GREAT
COURT &
READING
ROOM

1 Rosetta Stone
2 Upper Half of Ramesses II
3 Egyptian Gods as Animals
4 Monumental Granite Scarab
5 Up to Nebamun Hunting in
the Marshes
6 Up to Mummies, Coffins, Etc.

7 Red Granite Head
8 Four Black Granite Figures
9 Limestone Fragment of
Sphinx Beard
10 Limestone False Door &
Architrave of Ptahshepses
11 Statue of Nenkheftka

The Rosetta Stone allowed scientists to break the code. It contains a single inscription repeated in three languages. The bottom third is plain old Greek (find your favorite frat or sorority), while the middle is medieval Egyptian. By comparing the two known languages with the one they didn't know, translators figured out the hieroglyphics.

The breakthrough came when they discovered that the large ovals (e.g., in the sixth line from the top) represented the name of the ruler, Ptolemy. Simple.

▶ *The Rosetta Stone sits in the middle of the long Egyptian Gallery. In the gallery to the right of the Stone, find the huge head of Ramesses.*

2 Upper Half of Colossal Statue of Ramesses II of Granite (c. 1270 B.C.)
When Moses told the king of Egypt, "Let my people go!" this was the stony-faced look he got. Ramesses II ruled for 66 years (c. 1290–1223 B.C.) and may have been in power when Moses (as the Bible says) cursed Egypt

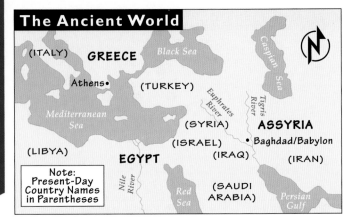

The Ancient World

(ITALY) **GREECE** Black Sea

Caspian Sea

Athens•

(TURKEY)

Euphrates River

Tigris River

Mediterranean Sea

(SYRIA) **ASSYRIA**

• Baghdad/Babylon

(LIBYA) **EGYPT** (ISRAEL)

(IRAQ) (IRAN)

Nile River

Red Sea

(SAUDI ARABIA)

Persian Gulf

Note: Present-Day Country Names in Parentheses

with plagues, freed the Israeli slaves, and led them out of Egypt to their homeland in Israel. This seven-ton statue, made from two different colors of granite, is a fragment from a temple in Thebes. It shows Ramesses with the traditional features of a pharaoh—goatee, cloth headdress, and cobra diadem on his forehead. Ramesses was a great builder of temples, palaces, tombs, and statues of himself. There are probably more statues of him in the world than there are cheesy fake *Davids*. He was so concerned about achieving immortality that he even chiseled his own name on other people's statues. Very cheeky.

▶ *Climb the ramp behind Ramesses, looking for animals.*

❸ Egyptian Gods as Animals

The Egyptians worshipped animals as incarnations of the gods. The powerful ram is the god Amun (king of the gods), protecting a puny pharaoh under his powerful chin. The falcon is Horus, the god of the living. The speckled, standing hippo (with lion head) is Tawaret—pregnant and grimacing in labor as the protectress of childbirth. Finally, the cat (with ear- and nose-rings) served Bastet, the popular goddess of stress relief.

▶ *At the end of the Egyptian Gallery—past several large stone coffins—is a big stone beetle.*

❹ Monumental Granite Scarab (c. 200 B.C.)

This species of beetle would burrow into the ground, then reappear—like the sun rising and setting, or dying and rebirth, a symbol of resurrection. Scarab amulets were placed on mummies' chests to protect the spirit's heart from acting impulsively. Pharaohs wore the symbol of the beetle, and tombs and temples were decorated with them. The hieroglyph for scarab meant "to come into being."

▶ You can't call Egypt a wrap until you visit the mummies upstairs. Continue to the end of the gallery past the giant stone scarab and up the West Stairs (four flights). At the top, take a left into Room 61, with objects and wall-paintings from the tomb of Nebamun.

❺ Painting of Nebamun Hunting in the Marshes (c. 1425 B.C.)

Nebamun stands in a reed boat, gliding through the marshes. He raises his arm, ready to bean a bird with a snakelike hunting stick.

This nobleman walks like Egyptian statues look—stiff and flat, like he was just run over by a pyramid. We see the torso from the front and everything else—arms, legs, face—in profile, creating the funny walk that has become an Egyptian cliché.

But the stiffness is softened by a human touch. It's a snapshot of a family outing. On the right, his wife looks on, while his daughter crouches between his legs, a symbol of fatherly protection. There's even the family cat (thigh-high, in front of the man) acting as a retriever—possibly the only cat in history that ever did anything useful.

When Nebamun passed into the afterlife, his awakening soul could look at this painting on the tomb wall and think of his loved ones for all eternity.

Scarab—beetle symbolizing rebirth

Nebamun—surprisingly realistic family scene

▶ *Browse through Rooms 61–64, filled with displays in glass cases.*

❻ Rooms 61–64: Mummies, Coffins, Canopic Jars, and Statuettes— The Egyptian Funeral

To mummify a body: disembowel it (but leave the heart inside), pack the cavities with pitch, and dry it with natron, a natural form of sodium carbonate (and, I believe, the active ingredient in Twinkies). Then carefully bandage it head to toe with hundreds of yards of linen strips. Let it sit 2,000 years, and...*voilà!*

The mummy was placed in a wooden coffin, which was put in a stone coffin, which was placed in a tomb. (The pyramids were super-sized tombs for the rich and famous.) The result is that we now have Egyptian bodies that are as well preserved as Joan Rivers.

The internal organs were preserved alongside in canopic jars, and small-scale statuettes of the deceased *(shabtis)* were scattered around. Written in hieroglyphs on the coffins and the tomb walls were burial rites from the Book of the Dead. These were magical spells to protect the body and crib notes for the waking soul, who needed to know these passwords to get past the guardians of eternity.

Browse these rooms, noticing the Roman-era portraits of the deceased and the mummies of cats (Room 62). Worshipped in life as the sun god's allies, preserved in death, and memorialized with statues, cats were given the adulation they've come to expect ever since.

▶ *In Room 64, in a glass case, you'll find what's left of a visitor who tried to see the entire museum in one visit. (Actually, it's the body of a man called...)*

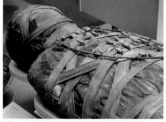
Mummy—preserving bodies for the afterlife

"Ginger"—5,400-year-old corpse

"Ginger" (Typical Egyptian Grave Containing a Naturally Preserved Body)
This man died 5,400 years ago, a thousand years before the pyramids. His people buried him in the fetal position, where he could "sleep" for eternity. The hot sand naturally dehydrated and protected the body. With him are a few of his possessions: bowls, beads, and the flint blade next to his arm. His grave was covered with stones. Named "Ginger" by scientists for his wisps of red hair, this man from a distant time seems very human.

▶ *Backtrack to Room 61 and head back down the stairs to the Egyptian Gallery and the Rosetta Stone. Just past the Rosetta Stone, find a huge head (facing away from you) with a hat like a bowling pin.*

⑦ Red Granite Head from a Colossal Figure of a King (c. 1350 B.C.)
Art also served as propaganda for the pharaohs, kings who called themselves gods on earth. Put this head on top of an enormous body (which still stands in Egypt), and you have the intimidating image of an omnipotent ruler who demands servile obedience. Next to the head is, appropriately, the pharaoh's powerful fist—the long arm of the law. The crown is actually two crowns in one. The pointed upper half is the royal cap of Upper Egypt. This rests on the flat, fez-like crown symbolizing Lower Egypt. A pharaoh wearing both crowns together is bragging that he rules a combined Egypt.

▶ *Along the wall to the left of the red granite head (as you're facing it) are four black lion-headed statues.*

⑧ Four Black Granite Figures of the Goddess Sakhmet (1400 B.C.)
This lion-headed goddess Sakhmet looks pretty sedate here, but she could spring into a fierce crouch when crossed. She was the pharaoh's personal bodyguard, who could burn his enemies to a crisp with flaming

Red Granite Head—fragment of a colossus

Sakhmet—the lion-headed goddess

arrows. Sakhmet holds an ankh. This key-shaped cross was the hiero-glyph meaning "life" and was a symbol of eternal life. Later, it was adopted as a Christian symbol because of its cross shape and religious overtones.

▶ *Continuing down the Egyptian Gallery, a few paces directly in front of you and to the left, find a glass case containing a...*

❾ Limestone Fragment of the Beard of the Sphinx

The Great Sphinx—a statue of a pharaoh-headed lion—crouches in the shadow of the Great Pyramids in Cairo. Time shaved off the sphinx's soft-sandstone, goatee-like beard, and a piece is now preserved here in a glass case. This hunk of stone is only a whisker—about three percent of the massive beard—giving an idea of the scale of the six-story-tall, 250-foot-long statue.

▶ *Ten steps past the Sphinx's soul patch is a 10-foot-tall, red-tinted "build-ing" covered in hieroglyphics.*

❿ Limestone False Door and Architrave of Ptahshepses (c. 2400 B.C.)

This "false door" was a ceremonial entrance (never meant to open) for a sealed building, called a *mastaba,* that marked the grave of a man named Ptahshepses. The hieroglyphs of eyes, birds, and rabbits serve as his epitaph, telling his life story, how he went to school with the pharaoh's kids, became an honored administrator, and married the pharaoh's daughter.

The deceased was mummified, placed in a wooden coffin that was encased in a stone coffin, then in a stone sarcophagus (like the **red-granite sarcophagus with paneled exterior surfaces** in front of Ptahshepses' door), and buried 50 feet beneath the *mastaba* in an underground cham-ber (see the diagram of "Old Kingdom Tombs," on a nearby wall).

Mastabas like Ptahshepses' were decorated inside and out with stat-ues, stelas, and frescoes like those displayed nearby. These pictured the things that the soul could find useful in the next life—magical spells, lists of the deceased's accomplishments, snapshots of the deceased and his family while alive, and secret passwords from the Egyptian Book of the Dead. False doors like this allowed the soul—but not grave robbers—to come and go.

Limestone false door—spirits enter here

Nenkheftka's soul takes a walk.

▸ *Just past Ptahshepses' false door is a glass case with a statue.*

⑪ Statue of Nenkheftka (2400 B.C.)
Originally standing in a "false door" of his *mastaba,* this statue represented the soul of the deceased still active, going in and out of the burial place. This was the image of the departed that greeted his loved ones when they brought food offerings to the *mastaba* to place at his feet to nourish his soul. (In the mummification rites, the mouth was ritually opened, to prepare it to eat soul food.)

In ancient Egypt, you *could* take it with you. After you died, your soul lived on, enjoying its earthly possessions—sometimes including servants, who might be walled up alive with their master. (Remember that even the great pyramids were just big tombs for Egypt's most powerful.)

Statues functioned as a refuge for the soul on its journey after death. The rich scattered statues of themselves everywhere, just in case. Statues needed to be simple and easy to recognize, mug shots for eternity: stiff, arms down, chin up, nothing fancy. This one has all the essential features, like the stylized human figures on international traffic signs. To a soul caught in the fast lane of astral travel, this symbolic statue would be easier to spot than a detailed one.

With their fervent hope for life after death, Egyptians created calm, dignified art that seems built for eternity.

▸ *Relax. One civilization down, two to go. Near the end of the gallery are two huge, winged Assyrian lions (with bearded human heads) standing guard over the Assyrian exhibit halls.*

Assyria (900–600 B.C.)

Long before Saddam Hussein, Iraq was home to other palace-building, iron-fisted rulers—the Assyrians.

Assyria was the lion, the king of beasts of early Middle Eastern civilizations. This Semitic people from the agriculturally challenged hills of northern Iraq became traders and conquerors, not farmers. They conquered their southern neighbors and dominated the Middle East for 300 years (c. 900–600 B.C.).

Their strength came from a superb army (chariots, mounted cavalry, and siege engines), a policy of terrorism against enemies ("I tied their heads to tree trunks all around the city," reads a royal inscription), ethnic cleansing and mass deportations of the vanquished, and efficient administration (roads and express postal service). They have been called "The Romans of the East."

Two Human-Headed Winged Lions (c. 865–860 B.C.)

These lions guarded an Assyrian palace. With the strength of a lion, the wings of an eagle, the brain of a man, and the beard of ZZ Top, they protected the king from evil spirits and scared the heck out of foreign ambassadors and left-wing newspaper reporters. (What has five legs and flies? Take a close look. These quintupeds, which appear complete from both the front and the side, could guard both directions at once.)

Carved into the stone between the bearded lions' loins, you can see one of civilization's most impressive achievements—writing. This wedge-shaped (cuneiform) script is the world's first written language, invented 5,000 years ago by the Sumerians (of southern Iraq) and passed down to their less-civilized descendants, the Assyrians.

Assyrian winged lions standing guard

Assyrian King—a powerful conquerer

British Museum—Assyria

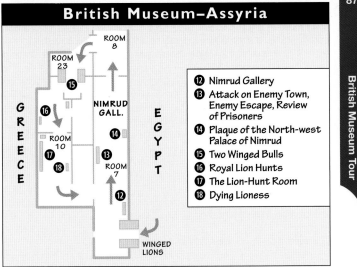

12 Nimrud Gallery

13 Attack on Enemy Town, Enemy Escape, Review of Prisoners

14 Plaque of the North-west Palace of Nimrud

15 Two Winged Bulls

16 Royal Lion Hunts

17 The Lion-Hunt Room

18 Dying Lioness

▶ *Walk between the lions, glance at the large reconstructed wooden gates from an Assyrian palace, and turn right into the long, narrow red gallery (Room 7) lined with brown relief panels.*

12 Nimrud Gallery (Ninth Century B.C.)—Palace of Ashurnasirpal II

This gallery is a mini version of the throne room of King Ashurnasirpal II's palace at Nimrud (near modern-day Mosul). Entering, you'd see the king on his throne at the far end, surrounded by these pleasant, sand-colored, gypsum relief panels (which were, however, originally painted and varnished).

That's Ashurnasirpal himself in the **first panel on your right,** with braided beard, earring, fez-like crown, and bulging forearms, flanked by his supernatural hawk-headed henchmen, who sprinkle incense on him with pine cones. Ashurnasirpal II (r. 883–859 B.C.) was a conqueror's conqueror, and the room's panels chronicle his bloody career.

▶ *A dozen paces farther down, on the left wall, you'll find an upper panel labeled "Attack on an Enemy Town."*

⓭ Relief Panels

Attack on an Enemy Town: The Assyrians lay siege to a walled city with a crude "tank." It shields them as they smash down the gate with a battering ram. The king stands a safe distance away behind the juggernaut and bravely shoots arrows.

Enemy Escape: In the next panel to the right, enemy soldiers flee the slings and arrows of outrageous Assyrians by swimming across the Euphrates, using inflated animal bladders as life preservers. Their friends in the castle downstream applaud their ingenuity.

Review of Prisoners: Beneath that panel, a conquered nation is paraded before the Assyrian king, who is shaded by a parasol. Above the prisoners' heads, we see the spoils of war—elephant tusks, metal pots, etc.—that fueled the Assyrian economy. The Assyrian king sneers and tells the captured chief, "Drop and give me 50."

▶ *On the opposite wall, a few steps farther along, is an artist's rendering of what the palace would have looked like.*

⓮ Plaque of the North-West Palace of Nimrud

The plaque shows the king at the far end of the throne room, shaded by a parasol and flanked by winged lions. The 30,000-square-foot palace was built atop a 50-acre artificial mound.

▶ *Exit the Nimrud Gallery at the far end, then hang a U-turn left. Pause at the entrance of Room 10c to see the impressive...*

⓯ Two Winged Bulls from Khorsabad, the Palace of Sargon (c. 710–705 B.C.)

These marble bulls guarded the entrance to a vast palace complex built by Sargon II (r. 721–705 B.C.) near ancient Nineveh and Nimrud (modern Mosul). The 30-ton bulls were cut from a single block, tipped on their sides, then dragged to their place by POWs. In modern times, when the British transported them here, they had to cut them in half; you can see the horizontal cracks through the bulls' chests.

It was Sargon II who subdued the Israelites after a three-year siege of Jerusalem (2 Kings 17:1–6). He solidified his conquest by ethnically cleansing the area and deporting many Israelites, inspiring legends of the "Lost" Ten Tribes.

▶ *Sneak between these bulls and veer right (into Room 10), where lions, horses, and hunting dogs are resting peacefully, being readied for the* ⓰ *Royal Lion Hunts. Continue ahead into the larger lion-hunt room.*

Two winged bulls of Sargon

Reading the panels like a comic strip, start on the right and gallop counterclockwise.

⑰ The Lion-Hunt Room (c. 650 B.C.)—Panels from the Palace of Ashurbanipal

Lion hunting was Assyria's sport of kings. With staged hunts and zoo-bred lions, the kings of men proved their power by taking on the king of beasts.

They release the lions from their cages, then soldiers on horseback herd them into an enclosed arena. The Assyrian king (in the chariot) has them cornered. Having left a half-dozen corpses in his wake, he moves on, while spearmen hold off lions attacking from the rear.

▶ *At about the middle of the long wall...*

The fleeing lions, cornered by hounds, shot through with arrows, and weighed down by fatigue, begin to fall. The lead lion carries on even while vomiting blood.

▶ *On the wall opposite the vomiting lion is the...*

⑱ Dying Lioness

A lioness roars in pain and frustration. She tries to run, but her body is too heavy. Her muscular hind legs, once the source of her power, are now paralyzed.

This low point of Assyrian cruelty is, perhaps, the high point of their artistic achievement. It's a curious coincidence that civilizations often produce their greatest art in their declining years. Hmm.

Like these brave, fierce lions, Assyria's once-great warrior nation was slain. A generation after these panels were carved, Assyria was conquered, and their capital at Nineveh was sacked and looted (612 B.C.) by the Babylonians from modern Baghdad.

The mood of tragedy, dignity, and proud struggle in a hopeless cause makes this dying lioness simply one of the most beautiful of human creations.

▶ *Exit the lion-hunt room at the far end and make your way back to the huge, winged lions at the start of the Assyrian exhibit. To reach the Greek section, exit Assyria between the winged lions and make a U-turn to the right, into Room 11.*

You'll walk past ⑲ *early Greek Barbie and Ken dolls from the Cycladic*

Dying lioness—tragic art of a dying civilization

period (2500 B.C.). Continue into Room 12 (the hungry can go straight to the Gallery Café), and turn right, into Room 13, filled with Greek vases in glass cases. Pottery, mostly painted red and black, was a popular export product for the sea-trading Greeks.

Greece (600 B.C.–A.D. 1)

During its Golden Age (500–430 B.C.), Greece set the tone for all of Western civilization to follow. Democracy, theater, literature, mathematics, philosophy, science, gyros, art, and architecture, as we know them, were virtually all invented by a single generation of Greeks in a small town of maybe 80,000 citizens.

But Greece wasn't always Golden, and the museum traces the evolution of Greek art and culture, from crude and barbaric to sophisticated and civilized.

▶ *Roughly in the middle of Room 13 is a Z-shaped glass case marked #8. On the upper shelf, find a...*

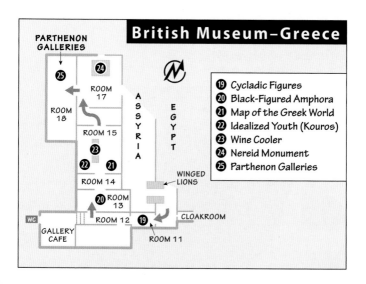

British Museum–Greece

PARTHENON GALLERIES

㉕   ㉔

ROOM 17

ROOM 18

ROOM 15

㉓

㉒   ㉑

ROOM 14

㉔   ROOM 13

WC   ROOM 12   ⑲

GALLERY CAFE   ROOM 11

A S S Y R I A

E G Y P T

WINGED LIONS

CLOAKROOM

⑲ Cycladic Figures
⑳ Black-Figured Amphora
㉑ Map of the Greek World
㉒ Idealized Youth (Kouros)
㉓ Wine Cooler
㉔ Nereid Monument
㉕ Parthenon Galleries

⑳ Black-Figured Amphora (Jar): Achilles and Penthesileia (540–530 B.C.)

Greeks poured wine from jars like this one, painted with a man stabbing a woman, a legend from the Trojan War.

Achilles of Greece (read his name "AXILEV") faces off against the Queen of the Amazons, Penthesileia ("PENOESIIEA"). Achilles bears down, plunging a spear through her neck, as the blood spurts. In her dying moment, Penthesileia looks up and her gaze locks on Achilles. His eyes bulge wide, and he falls instantly in love with her. She dies, and Achilles is smitten.

▶ *Continue to Room 15. On the entrance wall, find a...*

㉑ Map of the Greek World (500–430 B.C.)

After Greece drove out Persian invaders in 480 B.C., the city of Athens became the most powerful of the city-states and the center of the Greek world. By c. 330 B.C., the conqueror Alexander the Great had forged a Greek-speaking, "Hellenistic" empire that stretched from Italy and Egypt to India. Two hundred years later, this Greek-speaking world was conquered and assimilated by the Romans.

▶ *There's a nude male statue on the left side of the room.*

㉒ Idealized Youth (Kouros, 490 B.C.)

The Greeks saw their gods in human form...and human beings were

Achilles exchanges meaningful eye contact.

godlike. With his perfectly round head, symmetrical pecs, and navel in the center, the youth exemplifies the divine orderliness of the universe. The ideal statue was geometrically perfect, a balance between movement and stillness, between realistic human anatomy (with human flaws) and the perfection of a Greek god. This boy is still a bit uptight, stiff as the rock from which he's carved. But—as we'll see—in just a few short decades, the Greeks would cut loose and create realistic statues that seemed to move like real humans.

▶ *Two-thirds of the way down Room 15 (on the left) is a glass case containing a vase.*

㉓ Wine Cooler (Psykter) Signed by Douris as Painter (490 B.C.)

This clay vase, designed to float in a bowl of cooling water, shows satyrs at a symposium, or drinking party. These half-man/half-animal creatures (notice their tails) had a reputation for lewd behavior, reminding the balanced and moderate Greeks of their rude roots.

The reveling figures painted on this jar are impressively realistic, three-dimensional, and fluid. The Greeks are beginning to find the balance between stillness and motion. And speaking of "balance," if that's a Greek sobriety test, revel on.

▶ *Carry on into Room 17 and sit facing the Greek temple at the far end.*

Wine cooler—Greeks valued balanced art

㉔ Nereid Monument from Xanthos (c. 390–380 B.C.)

Greek temples (like this reconstruction of a temple-shaped tomb) were considered homes for the gods, with a statue of the god inside.

The triangle-shaped roof, filled in with sculpture, is called the "pediment." The cross beams that support the pediment are called "metopes" (MET-uh-pees). Now look through the columns to the building itself. Above the doorway is another set of relief panels running around the building (under the eaves), called the "frieze."

Next, we'll see pediment, metope, and frieze decorations from Greece's greatest temple.

▶ *Leave the British Museum. Take the Tube to Heathrow and fly to Athens. In the center of the old city, on top of the high, flat hill known as the Acropolis, you'll find...*

Nereid Monument—a mini-Parthenon

The Parthenon (447–432 B.C.)

The Parthenon—the temple dedicated to Athena, goddess of wisdom and the patroness of Athens—was the crowning glory of an enormous urban-renewal plan. After Athens was ruined in a war with Persia, the newly built Parthenon became the symbol of the Golden Age—a model of balance, simplicity, and harmonious elegance. Phidias, the greatest Greek sculptor, decorated the exterior (pediment, metopes, and frieze) with statues and relief panels.

While the building itself remains in Athens, many of the Parthenon's best sculptures are right here in the British Museum—the so-called Elgin Marbles (pronounced with a hard "g"), named for the shrewd British ambassador who hammered, chiseled, and sawed them off the Parthenon in the early 1800s. Though the Greek government complains about losing its marbles, the Brits feel they rescued and preserved the sculptures. The often bitter controversy continues.

▶ *Enter through the glass doors labeled* The Parthenon Galleries. *(The rooms branching off the entryway usually have helpful exhibits that reconstruct the Parthenon and its once-colorful sculpture.)*

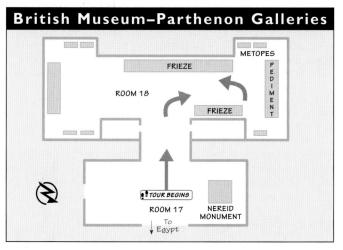

British Museum—Parthenon Galleries

METOPES

FRIEZE

PEDIMENT

ROOM 18

FRIEZE

TOUR BEGINS

ROOM 17

NEREID MONUMENT

To Egypt

The Parthenon temple in Athens

Elgin Marbles—stripped from Parthenon, now in London

㉕ Parthenon Galleries (450 B.C.)

The marble panels you see lining the walls of this large hall are part of the frieze that originally ran around the exterior of the Parthenon (under the eaves). The statues at either end of the hall once filled the Parthenon's triangular-shaped pediments. Near the pediment sculptures, we'll also find the relief panels known as metopes. Let's start with the frieze.

The Frieze

These 56 relief panels show Athens' "Fourth of July" parade, celebrating the birth of the city. On this day, citizens marched up the Acropolis to symbolically present a new robe to the 40-foot-tall gold-and-ivory statue of Athena housed in the Parthenon.

▶ *Start at the panels by the entrance (#136) and work counterclockwise.*

Men on horseback, chariots, musicians, children, animals for sacrifice, and young maidens with offerings are all part of the grand parade, all heading in the same direction—uphill. Prance on.

Notice the muscles and veins in the horses' legs and the intricate folds in the cloaks and dresses. Some panels have holes drilled in them, where gleaming bronze reins were fitted to heighten the festive look. All these panels were originally painted in realistic colors. As you move along, notice that, despite the bustle of figures posed every which way, the frieze has one unifying element—all the people's heads are at the same level, creating a single ribbon around the Parthenon.

▶ *Cross to the opposite wall.*

A three-horse chariot (#67), cut out of only a few inches of marble, is more lifelike and three-dimensional than anything the Egyptians achieved in a freestanding statue.

Enter the girls (five yards to the left, #61), the heart of the procession. Dressed in pleated robes, they shuffle past the parade marshals, carrying incense burners and jugs of wine and bowls to pour out an offering to the thirsty gods.

The procession culminates (#35) in the presentation of the robe to Athena. A man and a child fold the robe for the goddess while the rest of the gods look on. Zeus and Hera (#29), the king and queen of the gods, seated, enjoy the fashion show and wonder what length hemlines will be this year.

▶ *Head for the set of pediment sculptures at the far right end of the hall.*

The Pediment Sculptures

These statues were originally nestled nicely in the triangular pediment above the columns at the Parthenon's main (east) entrance. The missing statues at the peak of the triangle once showed the birth of Athena. Zeus

Frieze panels depict a parade.

had his head split open, allowing Athena, the goddess of wisdom, to rise from his brain fully grown and fully armed, inaugurating the Golden Age of Athens.

The other gods at this Olympian banquet slowly become aware of the amazing event. Hebe, the cup-bearer of the gods (tallest surviving fragment) runs to tell the others, her dress whipping behind her. The only one who hasn't lost his head is laid-back Dionysus (the cool guy farther left). He just raises another glass of wine to his lips. Over on the right, Aphrodite, goddess of love, leans back into her mother's lap. A chess-set horse's head screams, "These people are nuts—let me out of here!"

The scene had a message. Just as wise Athena rose above the lesser gods, who were scared, drunk, or vain, so would her city, Athens, rise above her lesser rivals.

This is amazing workmanship. Compare Dionysus, with his natural, relaxed, reclining pose, to all those stiff Egyptian statues standing eternally at attention. Appreciate the intricate folds of the clothes on the female figures. Even without their heads, these statues, with their detailed anatomy and expressive poses, speak volumes.

▶ *The metopes are the panels on the walls to either side. Start with the three South Metope panels on the right wall, center.*

Pediment—the gods lounge to the left...

The Metopes

The Metopes depict the battle between humans and centaurs. Metaphorically, they tell the story of Greece's own struggle to rise above nomadic barbarism to the pinnacle of early Western civilization.

In #XXXI, a centaur grabs a man by the throat while the man pulls his hair. The humans have invited some centaurs—wild half-man/half-horse creatures—to a wedding reception. The centaurs, the original party animals, get too drunk and try to carry off the women. A battle ensues. In #XXX, the centaur does the hair-pulling, and begins to drive the man to his knees.

In #XXVIII (opposite wall, center), the centaurs take control of the party, as one rears back and prepares to trample the helpless man. The leopard skin draped over the centaur's arm roars a taunt. The humans lose face.

In #XXVII (to the left), the humans rally. A centaur tries to run, but the man grabs him by the neck and raises his right hand (missing) to run him through.

The centaurs have been defeated. Civilization has triumphed over barbarism, order over chaos, and rational man over his half-animal alter ego.

...and right of Athena's amazing birth

Centaurs Slain Around the World

Dateline 500 B.C.—Greece, China, India: Man no longer considers himself an animal. Bold new ideas are exploding simultaneously around the world. Socrates, Confucius, Buddha, and others are independently discovering a nonmaterial, unseen order in nature and in man. They say man has a rational mind or soul. He's separate from nature and different from the other animals.

Why are the Parthenon sculptures so treasured? The British of the 19th century saw themselves as the new "civilized" race, subduing "barbarians" in their far-flung empire. Maybe these rocks made them stop and wonder—will our great civilization also turn to rubble?

▶ *Our tour is over, but of course there's much more to the British Museum.*

Pick up the free map to find the 2,000-year-old Lindow Man (Room 50), Anglo-Saxon treasures (Room 41), a Michelangelo sketch (Room 90), and the elegant Enlightenment Gallery (Room 1). Look for remnants

Metope #XXXI—centaurs battle humans

#XXX—centaurs get the upper hand

#XXVIII—centaurs triumph

#XXVII—humans rally, defeating the barbarians

of the sophisticated, exotic cultures of Asia and the Americas (North Wing) and Africa (lower floor)—all part of the totem pole of the human family.

EDUARDO PAOLOZZI · 1995

British Library Tour

The British Empire built its greatest monuments out of...paper. At the British Library, you'll see some of the many documents—literary, historical, and musical—that changed the course of history.

 These national archives of Britain include more than 12 million books, 180 miles of shelving, and the deepest basement in London. But everything that matters for our visit is in one delightful room, where we'll focus on the highlights. We'll stand before old maps, ancient Bibles, da Vinci's notebooks, the works of Shakespeare, highlights of English Lit 101, the Magna Carta, and—ladies and gentlemen—the Beatles.

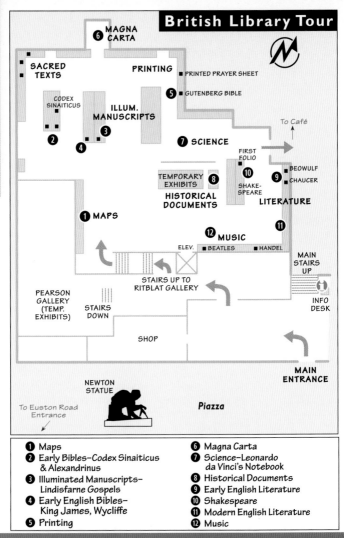

British Library Tour

1 Maps
2 Early Bibles–Codex Sinaiticus & Alexandrinus
3 Illuminated Manuscripts– Lindisfarne Gospels
4 Early English Bibles– King James, Wycliffe
5 Printing
6 Magna Carta
7 Science–Leonardo da Vinci's Notebook
8 Historical Documents
9 Early English Literature
10 Shakespeare
11 Modern English Literature
12 Music

ORIENTATION

Cost: Free, but £2 suggested donation. Temporary exhibits may have a separate (optional) charge.

Hours: Mon–Fri 9:30–18:00 (until 20:00 on Tue), Sat 9:30–17:00, Sun 11:00–17:00.

Getting There: It's at 96 Euston Road, a block west of Tube: King's Cross St. Pancras.

Information: Tel. 019/3754-6060. For questions on the collection, call 020/7412-7676 or go to www.bl.uk.

Tours: There are no guided tours or audioguides for "The Treasures." A free Rick Steves audio tour of the British Library is available on iTunes, Google Play, or at www.ricksteves.com.

Length of This Tour: Allow one hour.

Cloakroom: Free. For security, bags may be searched at the library entrance.

Photography: No photographs allowed.

Cuisine Art: The upper-level, self-service cafeteria has good hot meals. The ground-floor café has sandwiches and drinks. Both eateries have views of a 50-foot-tall wall of 65,000 books.

Newton statue at the entrance—a symbol of knowledge

THE TOUR BEGINS

Entering the library courtyard, you'll see a big statue of a naked Isaac Newton bending forward with a compass to measure the universe. The statue symbolizes the library's purpose: to gather all knowledge and promote our endless search for truth.

Stepping inside, you'll find our tour in a single, dimly lit room to the left. It's variously labeled "The Sir John Ritblat Gallery," "Treasures of the British Library," or just "The Treasures."

▶ *Enter and let your eyes adjust. The room has display cases grouped according to themes: maps to your left, sacred texts straight ahead, music to your right, and so on. Focus on the big picture, and don't be too worried about locating every specific exhibit in this tour—the displays change often. Start with our tour, then browse according to your interests.*

❶ Maps

The historic maps on the wall show how humans' perspective of the world expanded over the centuries. These pieces of paper, encoded with information gleaned from travelers, could be passed along to future generations—each building upon the knowledge of the last. A crude 13th-century map of Britain put medieval man in an unusual position—looking down on his homeland from 50 miles in the air. A few centuries later, maps of Britain were of such high quality they could be used today to plan a trip. And only a few generations after Columbus' first journey, the entire globe was fairly well-mapped, except for the mysterious expanse of unknown land that lay beyond America's east coast—"Terra Incognita."

▶ *Move into the area dedicated to sacred texts from several cultures—the Hebrew Torah, Muslim Quran, Buddhist sutras, and Hindu Upanishads. Start by browsing the different versions of the sacred text of Christians, the Bible.*

❷ Early Bibles—Codex Sinaiticus and Alexandrinus

My favorite excuse for not learning a foreign language is "If English was good enough for Jesus Christ, it's good enough for me!" I don't know what that has to do with anything, but obviously Jesus didn't speak English— nor did Moses or Isaiah or Paul or any other Bible authors or characters. As a result, our present-day English Bible came not directly from the mouths

Lindisfarne Gospels—copied and illustrated by monks

and pens of these religious figures, but is instead the fitful product of centuries of evolution and translation.

There are three things that editors must do in compiling the most accurate Bible: 1) decide which writings belong in the "anthology," 2) find the oldest and most accurate version (usually written in Hebrew or Greek), and 3) translate it accurately.

The **Codex Sinaiticus,** from A.D. 350, is one of the oldest complete Bibles in existence ("codex" means it's an ancient, bound manuscript). It's in Greek, the language in which most of the New Testament was written. The Old Testament portions are Greek translations from the original Hebrew. This particular Bible, and the nearby **Codex Alexandrinus** (A.D. 425), are old, but even they date from long after Jesus' death. Today, Bible scholars pore diligently over every word in the New Testament, trying to separate Jesus' authentic words from those that seem to have been added later.

❸ Illuminated Manuscripts—Lindisfarne Gospels

During Europe's Dark Ages after the fall of Rome, the Christian message was preserved by monks, who painstakingly reproduced ancient Bibles by hand. They wrote in Latin, the language of scholars ever since the Roman Empire. The Lindisfarne Gospels (A.D. 698) is the most magnificent of medieval British monk-uscripts. It's beautifully illustrated, or "illuminated," with elaborate tracery and interwoven decoration, mixing Irish, classical, and even Byzantine forms.

These Gospels are a reminder that Christianity almost didn't make it in Europe. After the fall of Rome (which had established Christianity as the Empire's official religion), much of Europe reverted to its pagan, tree-worshipping ways. Monasteries like the one at Lindisfarne (an island off the east coast of England) were the few beacons of light, tending the embers of civilization through the long night of the Dark Ages.

❹ Early English Bibles—King James Version, Wycliffe Bible, etc.

By the year 1400, the Bible was still written in Latin, even though only a small percentage of the population understood that language. A few brave reformers risked death to translate the sacred books into English.

These Bibles are written in the same language you speak, but try reading them. The strange letters and archaic words clearly show how quickly languages evolve. Jesus spoke Aramaic, a form of Hebrew. His words were written down in Greek. Greek manuscripts were translated into Latin, the language of medieval monks and scholars. In the 1400s, English scholars began translating the Greek and Latin into the King's English.

The King James version (made during his reign) has been the most widely used English translation. Fifty scholars worked for four years, borrowing heavily from previous translations, to produce the work. Its impact on the English language was enormous. It made Elizabethan English something of the standard, even after ordinary people had long since stopped saying "thee," "thou," and "verily, verily."

⑤ Printing — The Gutenberg Bible (c. 1455)

Printing was invented by the Chinese (what wasn't?). The **Printed Prayer Sheet** (c. 618–907) was printed using wooden blocks carved with Chinese characters, then dipped into paint or ink.

Johann Gutenberg (c. 1397–1468), a German silversmith, improved on the process. His Bible was the first book printed in Europe using movable type, one of the most revolutionary inventions in history.

Here's how it works: you scratch each letter onto a separate metal block, then arrange them into words, ink them up, and press them onto paper. When one job was done you could reuse the same letters for a new one.

Suddenly, the Bible was available for anyone to read, fueling the Protestant Reformation. Secular knowledge became accessible to a wide audience, fueling the Renaissance. Books were the mass medium of Europe, linking people by a common set of ideas.

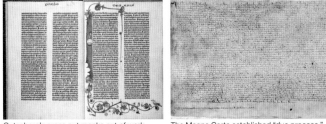

Gutenberg's press put monks out of work.

The Magna Carta established "due process."

❻ Magna Carta (1215)

Duck into the Magna Carta Room to answer this question: How did Britain, a tiny island with a few million people, come to rule a quarter of the world? Not by force, but by law. The Magna Carta was the basis for England's constitutional system of government. Though historians talk about "the" Magna Carta, several different versions of the document exist, some of which are kept in this room.

In 1215, England's barons rose in revolt against the slimy King John. (Remember, John appears as a villain in the legends of Robin Hood.) After losing London, John was forced to negotiate. The barons presented him with this list of demands. John, whose rule was worthless without the barons' support, had no choice but to affix his seal to it. Some 35 copies of the "Great Charter" were distributed around the kingdom.

This was a turning point in the history of government. Now, for the first time, there were limits—in writing—on how a king could treat his subjects. More generally, it established the idea of "due process"—the notion that a government can't infringe on citizens' freedom without a legitimate legal reason. This small step became the basis for all constitutional governments, including yours.

So what did this radical piece of paper actually say? The specific demands were trivial by today's standards—the king's duties to widows and orphans, inheritance taxes, and so on. But the principle—that the king had to abide by them as law—was revolutionary.

▶ *Now return to the main room to find...*

❼ Science—Leonardo da Vinci's Notebook

As books spread secular knowledge, Renaissance men turned their attention away from heaven and toward the nuts and bolts of the material world around them. These pages from Leonardo's notebook show his powerful curiosity, his genius for invention, and his famous backward and inside-out handwriting, which makes sense only if you know Italian and have a mirror. Leonardo's restless mind pondered diverse subjects, from how birds fly to the flow of the Arno River to military fortifications to an early helicopter to the "earthshine" reflecting onto the moon.

One person's research inspired another's, and books allowed knowledge to accumulate. Leonardo inspired Galileo, who championed the counter-commonsense notion that the earth spun around the sun. Galileo

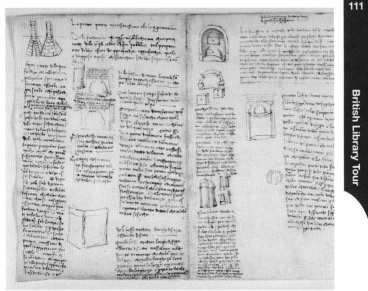

Leonardo's notebook

inspired Isaac Newton, who perfected the mathematics of those moving celestial bodies.

❽ Historical Documents

Nearby are many more historical documents. The displays change frequently, but you may see letters by Queen Elizabeth I, Darwin, Freud, Gandhi, and others. But for now, let's trace the evolution of...

❾ Early English Literature—*Beowulf* and *The Canterbury Tales*

Ponder this first English literary masterpiece, ***Beowulf***. The manuscript is from A.D. 1000, although the story itself dates to about A.D. 750. In this Anglo-Saxon story, the young hero Beowulf defeats two half-human monsters threatening the kingdom. Beowulf symbolizes England's emergence from the chaos and barbarism of the Dark Ages.

The poem is written in Old English, a language indecipherable to us today. Modern English is a mix derived from the various people who've inhabited the island: Celtic tribesmen, Latin-speaking Romans, German-speaking Anglos and Saxons (who named the island "Angle-land"—England), Vikings from Denmark, and French-speaking Normans under William the Conqueror. Four out of every five English words have been borrowed from other languages.

Six hundred years later, the island's inhabitants spoke Middle English. While most serious literature of the time was written in scholarly Latin, **The Canterbury Tales (c. 1410)** were written in the people's tongue. Geoffrey Chaucer's bawdy collection of stories, told by pilgrims on their way to Canterbury, gives us the full range of life's experiences—happy, sad, silly, sexy, and devout.

⑩ Shakespeare (1564–1616)

William Shakespeare is the greatest author in any language. Period. He expanded and helped define modern English. In one fell swoop, he made the language of everyday people as important as Latin. In the process, he gave us phrases like "one fell swoop," which we quote without knowing they're Shakespeare.

Perhaps as important was his insight into humanity. Think of his stock of great characters and great lines: Hamlet ("To be or not to be, that is the question"), Othello and his jealousy ("It is the green-eyed monster"), ambitious Mark Antony ("Friends, Romans, countrymen, lend me your ears"), rowdy Falstaff ("The better part of valor is discretion"), and the star-crossed lovers Romeo and Juliet ("But soft, what light through yonder window breaks"). Shakespeare probed the psychology of human beings 300 years before Freud. Even today, his characters strike a familiar chord.

William Shakespeare and Some Contemporaries: Some scholars have wondered whether Shakespeare—a journeyman actor with little education—actually wrote all these masterpieces. He was certainly surrounded by other great writers of the Elizabethan age, including his friend and fellow poet Ben Jonson. Most modern scholars, though, agree that Shakespeare did indeed write the plays and sonnets attributed to him.

The Shakespeare First Folio (1623): This published collection of his plays was the first authorized version. Shakespeare wrote his plays to be performed, not read. But as his reputation grew, unauthorized "bootleg" versions began to circulate. Some of these were shoddy, written by actors who were trying to re-create plays they had appeared in years before.

This folio, edited by friends and fellow actors, came out seven years after Shakespeare's death.

The title page has an engraving of Shakespeare, one of only two portraits done during his lifetime. The shiny, domed forehead is a beacon of intelligence. Is this what he really looked like? No one knows. The best answer probably comes from Ben Jonson, in the introduction on the facing page. Jonson concludes, "Reader, look not on his picture, but his book."

⓫ Modern English Literature

The rest of the "*Beowulf*/Chaucer wall" is a greatest-hits sampling of British literature, featuring works that have enlightened and brightened our lives for centuries. The displays rotate frequently, but there's always a tasty selection of famous works, from Austen to Carroll to Kipling to Woolf to Joyce to Dickens, whose novels were as popular in his time as blockbuster movies are today. In the 21st century, Britain continues to be a powerful force in the world of ideas and imagination.

⓬ Music

The Beatles: Bach, Beethoven, Brahms, Bizet...Beatles. Future generations will have to judge whether this musical quartet ranks with such artists, but no one can deny their historical significance. The Beatles burst onto the scene in the early 1960s to unheard-of popularity. With their long hair and loud music, they brought counterculture and revolutionary ideas to the middle class, affecting the values of a whole generation. Touring the globe, they served as a link between young people everywhere. Look for photos of John Lennon, Paul McCartney, George Harrison, and Ringo Starr before and after their fame.

Shakespeare, from the First Folio

Handel's *Messiah*

Most interesting are the manuscripts of song lyrics written by Lennon and McCartney, the two guiding lights of the group. "I Want to Hold Your Hand" was the song that launched them to superstardom. "A Hard Day's Night" and "Help" were title songs of two films capturing the excitement and chaos of their hectic touring schedule. Some call "A Ticket to Ride" the first heavy-metal song. "Michelle," with a line in French, seemed oh-so-sophisticated. "Yesterday," by Paul, was recorded with guitar and voice backed by a string quartet—a touch of class from producer George Martin. Also, glance at the rambling, depressed, and cynical but humorous "un-titled verse" by a young John Lennon. Is that a self-portrait at the bottom?

Handel's *Messiah* (1741) and Other Music Manuscripts: Kind of an anticlimax after the Fab Four, I know, but here are manuscripts by Mozart, Beethoven, Schubert, and others. George Frideric Handel's famous oratorio, the *Messiah,* was written in a flash of inspiration—three hours of music in 24 days. Here are the final bars of its most famous tune. Hallelujah.

St. Paul's Tour

No sooner was Sir Christopher Wren selected to refurbish Old St. Paul's Cathedral than the Great Fire of 1666 incinerated it. Within a week, Wren had a plan for a whole new building...and for the city around it, complete with some 50 new churches. For the next four decades he worked to achieve his vision—a spacious church, topped by a dome, surrounded by a flock of Wrens.

St. Paul's is England's national church. There's been a church on this spot since 604. It was the symbol of London's rise from the Great Fire of 1666 and of the city's survival of the Blitz of 1940. Today, it's a center of the Anglican faith, a living war memorial, and the final resting place of many great Londoners. Allow about an hour to see the church, plus another hour to climb the dome for expansive views, as we visit the spiritual heart of the City of London.

ORIENTATION

Cost: £16, includes church entry, dome climb, tour, and audioguide.

Hours: Mon–Sat 8:30–16:30, last church entry at 16:00, dome opens at 9:30, last entry at 16:15, closed Sun except for worship. Sometimes closed for special events—check the calendar at www.stpauls.co.uk for your specific visit.

Music and Services: Worship is free, but you can't sightsee or wander around before, during, or after services. Evensong service is Tue–Sat at 17:00 and Sun at 15:15. Other religious services are Mon–Sat at 8:00 and 12:30, and Sunday at 8:00, 10:15, 11:30, and 18:00.

Getting There: Located in The City, Tube: St. Paul's. Other nearby Tube stops are Mansion House, Cannon Street, and Blackfriars.

Information: Recorded info tel. 020/7236-4128, reception tel. 020/7246-8350, www.stpauls.co.uk.

Tours: Guided 90-minute tours are generally offered Mon–Sat at 10:45, 11:15, 13:30, and 14:00 (confirm schedule at 020/7246-8357). Guided tours and audioguides are included in admission. A free Rick Steves audio tour of St. Paul's is available on iTunes, Google Play, or at www.ricksteves.com.

Photography: No photography allowed.

Cuisine Art: A good café (£5 soups and sandwiches) and pricier restaurant are located in the crypt. The crypt also contains a fine gift shop and the WC.

Starring: Sir Christopher Wren, Wellington, and World War II.

Nearby: A helpful TI is located to the right of the church. Just behind the church is a modern shopping mall with great (free) views.

Approaching St. Paul's across the Millennium Bridge

Standing beneath St. Paul's rotunda

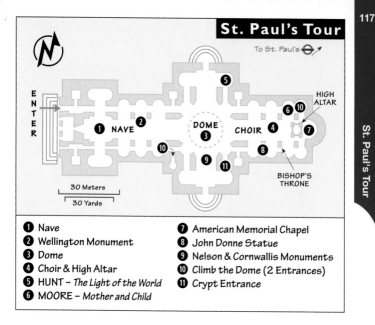

St. Paul's Tour

To St. Paul's ⊖

1 Nave
2 Wellington Monument
3 Dome
4 Choir & High Altar
5 HUNT – *The Light of the World*
6 MOORE – *Mother and Child*
7 American Memorial Chapel
8 John Donne Statue
9 Nelson & Cornwallis Monuments
10 Climb the Dome (2 Entrances)
11 Crypt Entrance

THE TOUR BEGINS

Even now, as skyscrapers encroach, the 365-foot-high dome of St. Paul's rises majestically above the rooftops of the neighborhood. The tall dome is set on classical columns, capped with a lantern, topped by a six-foot ball, and iced with a cross. As the first Anglican cathedral built in London after the Reformation, it is Baroque: St. Peter's in Rome filtered through clear-eyed English reason.

▶ *Enter, buy your ticket, pick up the free visitor's map, and stand at the far back of the nave.*

❶ Nave

Look down the nave through the choir stalls to the stained glass at the far end. At 515 feet long and 250 feet wide, it's Europe's fourth-largest, after Rome (St. Peter's), Sevilla, and Milan. It *feels* big. The spaciousness is accentuated by the relative lack of decoration. The simple, cream-colored ceiling and the clear glass in the windows light everything evenly. Wren wanted this: a simple, open church with nothing to hide.

Remarkably, this is the first great church completed in the lifetime of its architect (built 1675–1710). Unfortunately, only this entrance area keeps Wren's original vision—the rest was encrusted with 19th-century Victorian ornamentation.

▸ *Glance up and behind. The organ trumpets say, "Come to the evensong and hear us play." Ahead and on the left is the towering, black-and-white...*

❷ Wellington Monument

It's so tall that even Wellington's horse has to duck to avoid bumping its head. General Wellington, Napoleon's conqueror at Waterloo (1815) and the embodiment of British stiff-upper-lippedness, was honored here in a funeral packed with 13,000 fans. This church has become so central to England's soul that there are many memorials to national heroes, and many more are buried in the basement crypt.

▸ *Stroll up the same nave Prince Charles and Lady Diana walked on their 1981 wedding day. Imagine how they felt making the hike to the altar with the world watching. Grab a chair underneath the impressive dome.*

❸ The Dome

The dome is painted with scenes from the life of St. Paul. Those tiny tourists way up there walking around the base of the dome are in the Whispering Gallery, which we'll visit later.

The dome you see is only the innermost of three. Look up through the opening at the top to see the light-filled lantern of the second dome. Finally, the whole thing is covered on the outside by the third and final dome, the shell of lead-covered wood that you see from the street. Wren's ingenious three-in-one design was psychological as well as functional—he wanted a low, shallow inner dome so worshippers wouldn't feel diminished.

Christopher Wren (1632–1723) was the right man at the right time. Though the 31-year-old astronomy professor had never built a major building in his life when he got the commission for St. Paul's, his reputation for brilliance and his unique ability to work with others carried him through. The church has the clean lines and geometric simplicity of the

Wren's 365-foot dome defines London's skyline.

age of Newton, when reason was holy and God set the planets spinning in perfect geometrical motion.

For more than 40 years, Wren worked on this site, overseeing every detail of St. Paul's and the 65,000-ton dome. At age 75, he got to look up and see his son place the cross on top of the dome, completing the masterpiece.

On the floor directly beneath the dome is a brass grate. Encircling it is Christopher Wren's name and epitaph, written in Latin. It reads, *Lector, si monumentum requiris circumspice*—"Reader, if you seek his monument, look around you."

▶ *Look into the choir area toward the altar at the far end under a golden canopy.*

❹ The Choir and High Altar

English churches, unlike most in Europe, often have a central choir area (a.k.a. a "quire" or "chancel"), where church officials and the singers sit. St. Paul's—a cathedral since 604—is home to the local Anglican bishop, who presides in the chair nearest the altar on the south or right side (the chair marked by a carved bishop's hat hanging above).

The choir ceiling is a riot of glass mosaic representing God (above the altar) and eight angels showing off God's creation. These were added after Queen Victoria complained that Wren's original ceiling was "dreary and undevotional."

The altar (topped with crucifix and candlesticks) sits under a huge canopy with corkscrew columns. The canopy looks ancient, but it dates from 1958, when it was rebuilt after being heavily damaged in October 1940 by the bombs of Hitler's Luftwaffe.

▶ *In the north transept (to your left as you face the altar), find the big painting of Christ, in a golden wood altarpiece.*

❺ *The Light of the World* (1904), by William Holman Hunt

In the dark of night, Jesus—with a lantern, halo, jeweled cape, and crown of thorns—approaches an out-of-the-way home in the woods, knocks on the door, and listens for an invitation to come in. A Bible passage on the picture frame says: "Behold, I stand at the door and knock..." (Revelation 3:20).

In his early twenties, William Holman Hunt (1827–1910) was in the

The Anglican Communion

St. Paul's Cathedral is the symbolic (but not official) nucleus of earth's 70 million Anglicans. The Anglican Communion is a loose association of churches, including the Church of England and the Episcopal Church in the US.

Forged in the fires of Europe's Reformation, Anglicans see themselves as a "middle way" between Catholics and Protestants. They retain much of the pomp and ceremony of traditional Catholic worship but with Protestant elements such as married priests, attention to Scripture, and a less hierarchical approach to decision making.

The Church of England, the largest single body, is still the official religion of the state, headed by the Archbishop of Canterbury, who presides in Canterbury but lives in London. In 2010, Pope Benedict XVI visited London and met face to face with Archbishop Rowan Williams, signaling a new ecumenical spirit.

dark night of a spiritual crisis when he heard this verse knocking in his head. He opened his soul to Christ, his life changed forever, and he tried to capture the experience in paint. As one of the Pre-Raphaelites who adored medieval art, he used symbolism, but only images the average Brit-on-the-street could understand. The door is the closed mind, the weeds the neglected soul, the darkness is malaise, while Christ carries the lantern of spiritual enlightenment.

The critics savaged the painting—"syrupy," "too Catholic," "simple"—but the masses lapped it up. Its fame inspired countless Christ-at-the-door paintings in churches and homes. Hunt's humble-hippie image of Christ was stamped forever on the minds of generations of school kids. The painting became so famous that Hunt was asked to do this larger (second) version specifically for St. Paul's.

In the 21st century, *The Guardian* newspaper published a list of "Britain's Ten Worst Paintings." They compared *The Light of the World* to a plastic crucifix and honored it as number seven.

▶ *Return to the area underneath the dome and walk toward the altar, along the left side of the choir, pausing at a modern statue.*

Moore's sculpture—abstract but affecting

The American Memorial Chapel book honors WWII heroes.

❻ *Mother and Child,* by Henry Moore

Britain's (and the world's?) greatest modern sculptor, Henry Moore, rendered a traditional subject in an abstract, minimalist way. This Mary and baby Jesus was inspired by the sight of British moms nursing babies in WWII bomb shelters. Moore intended the viewer to touch and interact with the art.

▶ *Continue to the altar at the far end of the church. The area behind it has three bright and modern stained-glass windows.*

❼ American Memorial Chapel

This special spot in St. Paul's honors the Americans who sacrificed their lives to save Britain in World War II. The stained glass windows even feature American iconography amid the saints. Spot the American eagle (center window, to the left of Christ), George Washington (right window, upper-right corner), and symbols of all 50 states. In the carved wood beneath the windows (far right panel), check out the tiny tree "trunk" (amid foliage, below the bird)—it's a US rocket ship circa 1958, shooting up to the stars.

Britain is very grateful to its WWII saviors, and remembers them religiously with the 500-page Roll of Honor, immediately behind the altar. It lists the 28,000 Yanks based in Britain who gave their lives during the war.

▶ *Continue around the altar and head back toward the entrance. On the left wall of the aisle, standing white in a black niche, is a statue of...*

St. Paul's, the Blitz, and the Battle of Britain

In the early days of World War II, the powerful Nazi army quickly overran Poland, Belgium, and France. A seemingly helpless Britain hunkered down, waiting to be invaded. Prime Minister Winston Churchill vowed, "We shall fight on the beaches... We shall fight in the fields and in the streets... We shall never surrender."

Britain fought back. Daring squadrons of British Spitfire airplanes—aided by a secret weapon, radar—shot down 1,700 German planes. By September 1940, the German invasion was called off, and the "Battle of Britain" was won.

A frustrated Hitler retaliated with a series of punishing air raids on London itself, known as "the Blitz." All through the fall, winter, and spring of 1940–1941, including 57 consecutive nights, Hermann Göring's Luftwaffe pummeled a defenseless London, killing 20,000 and leveling half the city. Residents took refuge deep in the Tube stations. From his Whitehall bunker, Churchill made radio broadcasts exhorting his people to give their all, their "blood, toil, sweat, and tears."

On December 29, 1940, some 28 bombs fell on St. Paul's. The surrounding neighborhood was absolutely flattened, but the church rose above it, nearly intact. Some swear that many bombs bounced miraculously off Wren's dome. (Others credit the heroic work of local firefighters.) The church did suffer two direct hits, crumbling the altar and collapsing the north transept. But its survival gave hope to London's citizens. Britain's resolve had returned, the pendulum shifted, and the Nazis were defeated.

After the war, St. Paul's was the site of Churchill's state funeral, a bittersweet remembrance. In London's darkest time, Churchill had said that even if the empire lasted a thousand years, Britons would look back and say, "This was their finest hour."

❽ John Donne (1573–1631)

This statue survived the Great Fire of 1666. John Donne, shown here wrapped in a burial shroud, was a passionate preacher in old St. Paul's (1621–1631), as well as a great poet.

Imagine hearing Donne deliver a funeral sermon here, with the huge church bell tolling in the background: "No man is an island....Any man's death diminishes me, because I am involved in Mankind. Therefore, never wonder for whom the bell tolls—it tolls for thee."

▸ *And also for dozens of people who lie buried beneath your feet, in the crypt where you'll end your tour. But first, in the south transept, find the...*

❾ Horatio Nelson Monument and Charles Cornwallis Monument

Admiral Horatio Nelson (1758–1805) leans on an anchor, his coat draped discreetly over the arm he lost in battle.

In October 1805, England trembled in fear as Napoleon—bent on world conquest—prepared to invade from across the Channel. Meanwhile, hundreds of miles away, off the coast of Spain, the daring Lord Nelson's fleet smashed the French navy at Trafalgar, and Napoleon's hopes for a naval invasion of Britain sank. Unfortunately, Nelson took a sniper's bullet in the spine and died, gasping, "Thank God I have done my duty." The lion at Nelson's feet groans sadly, and two little boys gaze up—one at Nelson, one at Wren's dome. You'll find Nelson's tomb directly beneath the dome, downstairs in the crypt.

Opposite Nelson is a man Yanks will recognize. Charles Cornwallis (1738–1805) was the general who surrendered to George Washington at Yorktown in 1780. That ended the Revolutionary War, or as they call it over here—the "American War."

"Whispering Gallery"

The hero Nelson lies beneath the dome.

▶ *There are several entrances to the dome and its Galleries, but only one is open to the public at any given time, so check the free visitor's map.*

❿ Climb the Dome

It's 528 steps to the top—no elevator. Allow an hour to go up and down. The tower has three levels, called galleries, and each offers something different. The climb gets steeper, narrower, and more claustrophobic as you go higher. It's a one-way system, so you can't come back down until you reach the next level.

After 257 steps, you first reach the Whispering Gallery, with nice views of the church interior. The dome is constructed with such acoustic precision that sweet nothings whispered from one side of the dome can be heard on the opposite side, 170 feet away. Exactly how it works is debated—some even question *if* it works. Most likely, the sound does not travel up and over the dome to the diametrically opposite side, as it would

The view from the Dome, looking east, includes Tower 42 (far left) and bullet-shaped 30 St. Mary Axe.

in a perfect sphere. Rather, it goes around the curved wall horizontally, so you don't have to stand directly opposite each other to get results. For best effects, try whispering (not talking) with your mouth close to the wall, while your partner stands a few dozen yards away with their ear to the wall.

After another set of stairs, you're at the Stone Gallery, offering expansive views of London. If you're exhausted, claustrophobic, or wary of heights, this middle level might be high enough. (The top level has very little standing room for tourists.)

Finally a long, tight, metal staircase takes you to the very top of the cupola, the Golden Gallery. (Just before the final dozen stairs to the top, there's a tiny window at your feet that allows you to peek directly down—350 feet—to the church floor.) Once at the top, you emerge to stunning unobstructed views of the city. Looking west, you'll see the London Eye and Big Ben. To the south, across the Thames, is the rectangular smokestack of the Tate Modern, with Shakespeare's Globe nestled nearby.

To the east is the 600-foot-tall, black-topped Tower 42 and the bullet-shaped 30 St. Mary Axe building (nicknamed "The Gherkin"). Looking farther into the distance, the cluster of skyscrapers marks Canary Wharf. Just north of that is the area built for the 2012 Olympic Games. As you survey the teeming, fast-growing expanse of the East End and the Docklands, you're looking into London's future.

▶ *Descend the dome to church level, then follow signs directing you downstairs to the...*

⑪ Crypt

Many famous people are buried here. Start by locating the central tomb of Horatio Nelson, who wore down Napoleon. It's a big coffin-on-a-pedestal in a round alcove at the center of the crypt, directly beneath the dome. Nearby is the tomb of the Duke of Wellington, who finished Napoleon off. Use the free visitor's map to find other tombs: the painters Turner and Reynolds, Florence Nightingale, and a memorial to George Washington (who lies buried back in old Virginny).

To find the tomb of Christopher Wren, head up the central axis of the crypt, through the chapel, and turn right at the chapel's altar. The man who built this glorious cathedral is buried beneath it, in a humble grave marked with just a plain black slab, with no statue. "If you seek his monument... look around you."

Tower of London Tour

William I, still getting used to his new title of "the Conqueror," built a castle tower here (1077–1097) to keep the Londoners in line. Over the centuries, his successors built more walls and towers around it to create this complex, which today covers 18 acres. The heavily fortified Tower served as a royal residence, the Royal Mint, the Royal Jewel House, and, most famously, as the prison and execution site of those who dared oppose the Crown.

The Tower represents the ultimate power of the monarch. See the execution site where Henry VIII axed exes. Ogle the crown jewels, the richest on earth. See prisons that held the likes of Sir Walter Raleigh, Queen Elizabeth, and the Nazi Rudolf Hess. Tour halls of armor and weapons and take a meaty Beefeater tour. You'll find more bloody history per square inch than anywhere else in Britain by touring this original tower of power.

Tower of London Tour

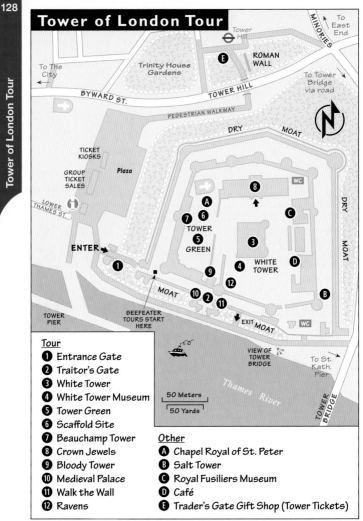

To East End

MINORIES

Tower HILL

To The City

ROMAN WALL

Trinity House Gardens

E

To Tower Bridge via road

BYWARD ST.

TOWER HILL

PEDESTRIAN WALKWAY

DRY MOAT

N

TICKET KIOSKS

Plaza

GROUP TICKET SALES

DRY MOAT

LOWER THAMES ST.

WC

8

A

C

7 **6**

TOWER

5 GREEN

3

WHITE TOWER

D

ENTER

1

9

4

MOAT

12

10 **2** **11**

B

TOWER PIER

BEEFEATER TOURS START HERE

EXIT MOAT

WC

VIEW OF TOWER BRIDGE

To St. Kath. Pier

Thames River

50 Meters

50 Yards

TOWER BRIDGE

Tour

1. Entrance Gate
2. Traitor's Gate
3. White Tower
4. White Tower Museum
5. Tower Green
6. Scaffold Site
7. Beauchamp Tower
8. Crown Jewels
9. Bloody Tower
10. Medieval Palace
11. Walk the Wall
12. Ravens

Other

A Chapel Royal of St. Peter
B Salt Tower
C Royal Fusiliers Museum
D Café
E Trader's Gate Gift Shop (Tower Tickets)

ORIENTATION

Cost: £22.

Hours: March–Oct Tue–Sat 9:00–17:30, Sun–Mon 10:00–17:30; Nov–Feb Tue–Sat 9:00–16:30, Sun–Mon 10:00–16:30; last entry 30 minutes before closing.

Advance Tickets: To avoid the long ticket-buying lines, buy your ticket at the Trader's Gate gift shop, located at the Tower Hill Tube stop. (As you exit the station, go down a flight of steps—the low-profile souvenir store is tucked away at the foot of the stairs.) You can also buy tickets at the Tower Welcome Centre (to the left of the normal ticket lines), by phone (tel. 0844-482-7799 within UK or tel. 011-44-20-3166-6000 from the US, £2 fee), or online (www.hrp.org.uk, £1 discount, no fee).

More Crowd-Beating Tips: It's most crowded in summer, on weekends (especially Sundays), and during school holidays. Avoid lines at the always crowded crown jewels by visiting before 10:00 or after 16:30.

Getting There: The Tower is located in East London (Tube: Tower Hill). Thames Clipper boats make the pleasant 30-minute trip from Westminster Pier near Big Ben.

Information: Switchboard toll tel. 0844-482-7777, www.hrp.org.uk.

Yeoman Warder (Beefeater) Tours: The free, one-hour Beefeater tours leave about every 30 minutes from inside the gate (last one at 15:30, 14:30 in winter). The boisterous Beefeaters are great entertainers, focusing on bloody anecdotes. If pleased, you can tip your Beefeater a coin (not a bill) at the end. Audioguides are £4.

Length of This Tour: Allow two hours.

Photography: Photos are allowed, except of the jewels or in the chapels.

Cuisine Art: The New Armouries Café, inside the Tower, is a big, efficient cafeteria (large, splittable meals for £8). Outside the Tower, there's an Apostrophe food shop along the river; the big, modern Eat, uphill from the ticket lines; and various take-out stands. Picnicking is allowed on the Tower grounds.

Starring: Crown jewels, Beefeaters, William the Conqueror, and Henry VIII.

THE TOUR BEGINS

❶ Entrance Gate

Even an army the size of the ticket line couldn't storm this castle. After the drawbridge was pulled up and the iron portcullis slammed down, you'd have to swim a 120-foot moat; cross an island prowled by wild animals; then toss a grappling hook onto a wall and climb up while the enemy poured boiling oil on you. If you made it this far, you'd only be halfway there.

You'd still have to swim a second moat—eventually drained to make the grassy parade ground we see today—then, finally, scale a second, higher wall. In all, the central tower was surrounded by two concentric rings of walls. Yes, it was difficult to get into the Tower (if you were a foreign enemy)...but it was almost as impossible to get out (if you were an enemy of the state).

▶ *Show your ticket, enter, pick up a free map, and check the posted schedule of Beefeater tours and daily events. When you're all set, go 50 yards straight ahead to the...*

❷ Traitor's Gate

This was the boat entrance to the Tower from the Thames. Princess Elizabeth, who was a prisoner here before she became Queen Elizabeth I, was carried down the Thames and through this gate on a barge, thinking about her mom, Anne Boleyn, who had been decapitated inside just a few years earlier. Many English leaders who fell from grace entered through here—Elizabeth was one of the lucky few to walk out.

▶ *Pass underneath the "Bloody Tower" into the inner courtyard. The big, white tower in the middle is the...*

Some of the Tower's many ramparts

Traitor's Gate—the boat entrance

The Beefeaters

The original duty of the Yeoman Warders (called "Beefeaters") was to guard the Tower, its prisoners, and the jewels. Their nickname may come from an original perk of the job—large rations of the king's beef. The Beefeaters dress in blue knee-length coats with red trim and a top hat. The "ER" on the chest stands for the monarch they serve—Queen Elizabeth II  (Elizabetha Regina in Latin). On special occasions, they wear red. All are retired officers from the armed forces with distinguished service records.

These days, the Yeoman Warders have evolved into charismatic tour guides. There are 35 Yeoman Warders, including one woman. They and their families make for a Beefeating community of 120 that live inside the Tower.

❸ White Tower

This square, 90-foot-tall tower is the original structure built by William the Conqueror that gave this castle complex of 20 towers its name. In the 13th century, the tower was painted white, hence the name.

Standing high above the rest of old London, the White Tower provided a gleaming reminder of the monarch's absolute power over subjects. If you made the wrong move here, you could be feasting on roast boar in the banqueting hall one night and chained to the walls of the prison the next. Torture ranged from stretching on the rack to the full monty: hanging by the neck until nearly dead, then "drawing" (cut open to be gutted), and finally quartering, with your giblets displayed on the walls as a warning. Any cries for help were muffled by the thick stone walls—15 feet at the base.

▶ *Either now or later, find time to go inside the White Tower for its excellent museum.*

White Tower—oldest of the Tower's towers

❹ White Tower Museum

Inside the White Tower, a one-way route winds through exhibits re-creating medieval life and the Tower's bloody history of torture and executions.

You'll see several suits of armor of Henry VIII—slender in his youth (c. 1515), heavy-set by 1540—with his bigger-is-better codpiece. Upstairs, the rare and lovely St. John's Chapel (1080) is where Lady Jane Grey (described later) offered up a last unanswered prayer. The Arsenal displays suits of armor of a 6'8" giant and a 3'1" midget (more likely a child), plus modern machine guns and the jeweled "Tiffany Revolver." On the top floor: there it is—the Tower's actual chopping block and execution ax.

▶ *Back outside, find the courtyard to the left of the White Tower, called...*

❺ Tower Green

This spacious courtyard within the walls was once the "town square" for those who lived in the castle. Knights exercised and jousted here, residents worshipped at the stone Chapel Royal of St. Peter ad Vincula (north side), and this was the last place of refuge in troubled times. The Tower is still officially a royal residence: the Queen's lodgings are on the south side of the green, in the white half-timbered buildings where a soldier stands guard.

▶ *Almost in the middle of the Tower Green is a granite-paved square marked Site of Scaffold.*

❻ Scaffold Site

The actual execution site looks pleasant enough today; the chopping block has been moved to inside the White Tower, and a modern sculpture encourages visitors to ponder those who died.

The White Tower Museum displays armaments.

The executioner's ax

Tower Green—the complex's courtyard

Execution site—Anne Boleyn died here

Here, enemies of the crown would kneel before the king for the final time. With their hands tied behind their backs, they would say a final prayer, then lay their heads on a block, and—*shlit*—the blade would slice through their necks, their heads tumbling to the ground. The headless corpses were buried in unmarked graves in the Tower Green or under the floor of the Chapel Royal of St. Peter ad Vincula. The heads were stuck on a stick and displayed at London Bridge. Passersby did not see heads, but spheres covered with insects and parasites.

Tower Green was the most prestigious execution site. Common criminals were hanged outside the Tower. More prominent evil-doers were decapitated before jeering crowds atop Tower Hill (near today's Tube station). Inside the Tower walls was reserved for the most heinous traitors.

Henry VIII axed a couple of his ex-wives here. (Divorced readers can insert their own cynical joke.) Anne Boleyn was the appealing young woman Henry had fallen so hard for that he broke with the Catholic Church in order to divorce his first wife and marry her. But when Anne failed to produce a male heir, she was locked up in the Tower, branded an adulteress and traitor, and decapitated.

Henry's fifth wife, teenage Catherine Howard, was also beheaded here. So was Jane Boleyn (Anne's sister-in-law) for arranging Catherine's adulterous affair behind Henry's back. Next.

In 1554, 17-year-old Lady Jane Grey—who'd been manipulated into claiming the crown—was executed here by her cousin Queen ("Bloody") Mary I. Young Jane had watched as her husband was decapitated hours earlier. Jane bravely blindfolded herself, hoping for a dignified end. But then she couldn't find the chopping block. She crawled around the scaffold pleading "Where is it?!" A bystander graciously helped her find it, thankfully avoiding a dreadful faux pas.

The Beefeaters, tired of "Hollywood coverage" of the Tower, often remind visitors that in more than 900 years, only 120 were executed here, and, of those, only six were executed inside the walls. Stressing the hospitality of the Tower, they insist that "Torture was actually quite rare here."

❼ The Beauchamp Tower—Prisoners

The Beauchamp Tower (pronounced "BEECH-um") was one of several places in the complex that housed Very Important Prisoners. In an upstairs room, you can read graffiti carved into the stone by bored and despondent inmates.

Picture Philip Howard, the Earl of Arundel (c. 1555–1595), warming himself by this fireplace and glancing out at the execution site during his 10-year incarceration. Having lived a devil-may-care life of pleasure in the court of Queen Elizabeth, the pro-Catholic Arundel was charged with treason by the Protestant government. He pleaded with the queen—his former friend—to at least let him see his wife and young children. She refused, unless he would renounce his faith.

On June 22, 1587, he carved his family name "Arundell" into the chimney (graffiti #13) and wrote in Latin, *Quanto plus afflictionis*—"The more we suffer for Christ in this world, the more glory with Christ in the next." Arundel suffered faithfully another eight years here before he wasted away and died at age 40.

Read other pitiful graffiti. Graffiti #85 belongs to Lady Jane Grey's young husband, Lord Guilford Dudley. Locked in the Beauchamp Tower and executed the same day as his wife, Dudley vented his despair by scratching "IANE" into the stone. Many prisoners held onto their sense of identity by carving their family's coats of arms.

The last enemy of state imprisoned in the Tower complex was one of its most infamous: the renegade Nazi Rudolf Hess. In 1941, Hitler's henchman secretly flew to Britain with a peace proposal (Hitler denied any such plan). He parachuted into a field, was arrested and held for four days in the Tower, and was later sentenced for war crimes.

▶ *Join the line leading to the crown jewels. Like a line for a Disney ride, the queue is still quite long even once you've made it in the door. But great videos help pass the time. First, you'll see a film of the Queen Elizabeth I's 1953 coronation, showing the jewels in use. Next comes*

Prisoners left pitiful messages.

The Crown Jewels

video close-ups of the jewels. After passing a hallway of ceremonial maces, swords, and trumpets, you finally reach...

❽ The Crown Jewels

The first displays show the royal regalia. The monarch-to-be is dressed in the 20-pound gold robe, anointed with holy oil poured from the eagle-beak flask, and handed the jeweled sword. The 12th-century coronation spoon, last used in 1953 to anoint the head of Queen Elizabeth, is the most ancient object here. Most of the original crown jewels from medieval times were lost during Cromwell's 1648 revolution.

After being dressed and anointed, the new monarch prepares for the "crowning" moment.

▶ *Five glass cases display the various crowns, orbs, and scepters used in various royal ceremonies. Ride the moving sidewalk that takes you past them. You're welcome to circle back and glide by again or hang out on the elevated viewing area.*

Scepter and Orb: After being crowned, the new monarch is handed these items. The Sovereign's Scepter is encrusted with the world's largest cut diamond—the 530-carat Star of Africa, beefy as a quarter-pounder. This was one of nine stones cut from the original 3,106-carat (1.37-pound) Cullinan diamond. The orb symbolizes how Christianity rules over the earth. The monarch is head of both the state and the Church of England.

St. Edward's Crown: This coronation crown is the one placed by the archbishop upon the head of each new monarch on coronation day in Westminster Abbey. It's worn for 20 minutes, then locked away until the next coronation. The original crown, destroyed by Cromwell, was older than the Tower itself and dated back to 1061, the time of King Edward the Confessor, "the last English king" before William the Conqueror invaded from France (1066). This 1661 remake is said to contain some of the original's gold amid its 443 precious and semiprecious stones. Because the crown weighs nearly five pounds, weak or frail monarchs have opted not to wear it.

Other Crowns: Among the several crowns, notice how four-arch crowns are for monarchs, while princes get only two.

The Crown of the Queen Mother: This crown, last worn by Elizabeth II's famous mum (who died in 2002), has the 106-carat Koh-I-Noor diamond glittering on the front. Since the diamond is considered unlucky for male rulers to wear, if Prince Charles becomes king, this crown might go to Camilla.

The **Queen Victoria Small Diamond Crown** is tiny. Victoria had a normal-sized head, but this was designed to sit atop the widow's veil she insisted on wearing for decades after the death of her husband, Prince Albert.

The **Imperial State Crown** is what the Queen wears for official functions such as the State Opening of Parliament. It's the crown depicted on Britain's coins and stamps. Among its 3,733 jewels are Queen Elizabeth I's former earrings (the hanging pearls, top center). The blue sapphire on top (in the center of the Maltese cross of diamonds) came from the ring of the King Edward the Confessor.

▶ *Leave the jewels by exiting through the thick vault doors. Back near the Traitor's Gate you'll find sights #9 and #10.*

❾ Bloody Tower

Not all prisoners died at the block. The 13-year-old future king Edward V and his kid brother were kidnapped in 1483 during the Wars of the Roses by their uncle Richard III ("Now is the winter of our discontent...") and locked in the Bloody Tower, never to be seen again (until two centuries later, when two children's skeletons were discovered).

Sir Walter Raleigh—poet, explorer, and political radical—was imprisoned here for 13 years. In 1603, the English writer and adventurer was accused of plotting against King James and sentenced to death. The king commuted the sentence to life imprisonment in the Bloody Tower. While in prison, Raleigh wrote the first volume of his *History of the World.* Check out his rather cushy bedroom, study, and walkway (courtesy of the powerful tobacco lobby?). Raleigh promised the king a wealth of gold if he would release him to search for El Dorado. The expedition was a failure. Upon Raleigh's return, the displeased king had him beheaded in 1618.

▶ *To reach the next sight, exit through the Bloody Gate, cross the cobbled road, and bear right a few steps to find the stairs up onto the wall.*

⑩ Medieval Palace

The Tower was a royal residence as well as a fortress. These rooms were built around 1240 by Henry III, the king most responsible for the expansive Tower of London complex we see today. You'll see the king's re-created bedroom and throne room, both with massive fireplaces to keep this cold stone palace cozy.

▶ *From the throne room, continue up the stairs to...*

⑪ Walk the Wall

Strolling the ramparts, you get a good look at the 13th century's state-of-the-art fortifications. You also can see the famous Tower Bridge, with the twin towers and blue spans. Although it looks somewhat medieval, this drawbridge was built in 1894 of steel and concrete. Sophisticated steam engines raise and lower the bridge, allowing tall ships to squeeze through.

Gaze out at the bridge, the river, City Hall (the egg-shaped glass building across the river), the Shard skyscraper (the city's bold new exclamation point), and life-filled London.

▶ *Between the White Tower and the Bloody Tower are cages housing the...*

⑫ Ravens

According to goofy tradition, London is only safe as long as the ravens are at the Tower. Their wings are clipped so they'll stay, and about ten are kept in the cage. World War II bombing raids reduced the population to one. In recent years, with their clipped wings, the birds had trouble mating, so a slide was built to help them get a bit of lift to mate. Happily, that worked, and a baby raven was born.

▶ *Take one final look at the stern stone walls of the Tower. Be glad you can leave.*

View of Tower (not "London") Bridge

Sights

London offers more world-class sights and museums than anyone could see in a single visit. To help you prioritize your limited time and money, I've clustered London's top sights into walkable neighborhoods for more efficient sightseeing. In the Westminster neighborhood, for example, you could string together a great day of sightseeing, linking Big Ben, Westminster Abbey, the Cabinet War Rooms, and much more. You'll find a full day's worth of sights in The West End, The City, the South Bank, and other neighborhoods.

Remember that some of London's biggest sights (marked with a ✪) are described in detail in the individual walks and tours chapters. See the Practicalities chapter for sightseeing tips.

And finally, remember that—although London's sights can be crowded and stressful—the city itself is all about gentility and grace under pressure. Be flexible.

Rick Steves' | Pocket London

CENTRAL LONDON

Westminster

In the shadow of Big Ben and Parliament, the Westminster neighborhood is Britain's government center. Most tourist sights lie in a half-mile stretch between Big Ben/Parliament (Tube: Westminster) and Trafalgar Square (Tube: Charing Cross).

▲▲Big Ben and the Houses of Parliament (Palace of Westminster)

This icon of London is where the British government's legislative branch meets.

Tourists can enter when Parliament is in session to see the impressive interior and view debates in either the bickering House of Commons or the genteel House of Lords. You must pass through security and be photographed. To avoid the hour-plus waits for the House of Commons, consider queuing up for the less-crowded, less-interesting, and less-powerful House of Lords. (Once inside, you can switch.)

▶ *Free. Usually open Mon–Tue 14:30–22:30, Wed 11:30–22:00, Thu 10:30–19:00. Closed Fri–Sun, with no sessions for most of Aug-Sept. No crowds after 18:00. Tube: Westminster. Tel. 020/7219-4272, check schedule at www.parliament.uk.*

✪ For more, see page 15 in the Westminster Walk chapter.

▲▲▲Westminster Abbey

✪ For a self-guided tour of Westminster Abbey, see page 29.

▲▲▲Churchill War Rooms

In the darkest days of World War II—with Nazi bombs raining down on a helpless London and invasion imminent—Britain's government hunkered down in this underground headquarters to direct the war effort. It was here that Prime Minister Winston Churchill lived, worked, and made stirring radio speeches that inspired Brits to carry on.

Today you can tour the well-preserved, 27-room, heavily fortified nerve center from 1939–1945. See Churchill's room, the map room, and other offices, while listening to recordings of first-person accounts. You'll see how British gentility survived even as the city was bombarded.

The Churchill Museum dissects every aspect of the man behind the famous cigar, bowler hat, and V-for-victory sign. You get a taste of

Winston's wit, irascibility, work ethic, passion for painting, American connections, writing talents, and drinking habits.

It traces the varied stages of his long life (1874–1965): newspaper reporter, war hero, Conservative politician, Liberal politician, and author. In the 1930s, he was a political pariah for ranting about the growing threat of Hitler's fascism. When his vision proved right, he was appointed Prime Minister on the day Hitler invaded the Netherlands. After the war, it was Churchill who warned of the Soviet threat, coining the phrase the "Iron Curtain." Touring this place, you have to wonder how different the world might have been today without Winston Churchill.

▶ *£16.50, excellent audioguide included. Open daily 9:30–18:00, last entry one hour before closing. Located on King Charles Street, 200 yards off Whitehall (Tube: Westminster). Food at the Switch Room café inside or the Westminster Arms Pub two blocks south on Storey's Gate. Tel. 020/7930-6961, www.iwm.org.uk.*

Horse Guards
✪ See page 24 in the Westminster Walk chapter.

▲Banqueting House

England's first classical-style building (1619–1622) has an impressive great hall topped with ceiling paintings by Peter Paul Rubens. Built as the dining hall and de facto throne room for King James I, it symbolized his "divine right" management style—the belief that God had anointed him to rule.

The hall is the only highlight of the visit—at 55 feet wide, 55 feet high, and 110 feet long, it's a perfect double cube.

The large, colorful ceiling paintings (up to 28 feet by 20 feet) portray James I as king of the whole world, crowned by Greek gods who bless him.

The Banqueting House's most famous role was as the place where James' son, Charles I, was executed—and divine-right rule ended. Today, it's a rent-a-hall hosting government receptions and concerts. You could even have your daughter's wedding reception here, with 400 guests and full catering, for as little as $100,000.

▶ *£5, includes dry audioguide. Open Mon–Sat 10:00–17:00, closed Sun, last entry at 16:30. Located along Whitehall (Tube: Westminster). Tel. 020/3166-6154 or 020/3166-6155, www.hrp.org.uk.*

✪ *For more on the exterior, see page 23 in the Westminster Walk chapter.*

On Trafalgar Square

▲▲Trafalgar Square
✪ See page 25 in the Westminster Walk chapter.

▲▲▲National Gallery
✪ See the National Gallery Tour on page 39.

▲▲National Portrait Gallery

Rock groupies, book lovers, movie fans, gossipmongers, and even historians all can find at least one favorite celebrity here. From Elizabeth I to Elizabeth II, Byron to Bowie, and Brontës to Beatles, the National Portrait Gallery is a *Who's Who* of 500 years of Britain's most fascinating people.

You'll see an imposing Henry VIII and several of his wives. Three different portraits of Elizabeth I offer multiple perspectives on the "Virgin Queen." William Shakespeare appears less as a stuffy scholar than a bohemian barfly. You'll see Charles I with his head on, Queen Victoria with her husband, writers in the throes of inspiration, and many scientists and philosophers who've changed the world.

The collection brings you right up to today, with sometimes-quirky portraits of the film stars, writers, and musicians that continue to make Britain great.

▶ *Free, but suggested donation of £5, optional temporary exhibits extra. Open daily 10:00–18:00, Thu–Fri until 21:00. Excellent themed audioguides, £3. The entrance is 100 yards off Trafalgar Square (Tube: Charing Cross or Leicester Square). Tel. 020/7306-0055, recorded info tel. 020/7312-2463, www.npg.org.uk.*

▲St. Martin-in-the-Fields

The church, built in the 1720s with a Gothic spire atop a Greek-type temple, is an oasis of peace on busy Trafalgar Square.

The church is famous for its concerts. Consider a free lunchtime concert (Mon, Tue, and Fri at 13:00), an evening concert (£8–28, several nights a week at 19:30), or Wednesday night jazz in the church's café (£5–10, at 20:00). See the website for the concert schedule.

A freestanding glass pavilion to the left of the church serves as the entrance to the church's underground areas: the concert ticket office, gift shop, brass-rubbing center, and the recommended Café in the Crypt.

▸ *Free, £3.50 audioguide at shop downstairs. Hours vary but generally open Mon–Fri 8:30–13:00 & 14:00–18:00, Sat 9:30–13:00 & 14:00–18:00, Sun 15:30–17:00. Tube: Charing Cross. Tel. 020/7766-1100, www.smitf.org.*

The West End and Nearby

Once located "west" of the medieval walled city of London, this area is now London's liveliest. Theaters, pubs, restaurants, shopping, museums, and nightlife abound. Leicester Square and Piccadilly Circus form the nucleus of this area. To the north lie London's Chinatown, the theatres of Shaftesbury Avenue, and the funky Soho neighborhood. Covent Garden and the shops of Regent Street are also nearby. The best Tube stops are Leicester Square and Piccadilly.

▲Leicester Square and Piccadilly Circus
✪ See page 64 in the West End Walk chapter.

▲Soho
✪ See page 67 in the West End Walk chapter.

▲▲Covent Garden
✪ See page 65 in the West End Walk chapter.

▲London Transport Museum

This modern, well-presented museum, located right at Covent Garden, is fun for kids and thought-provoking for adults. Whether you're cursing or marveling at the buses and Tube, the growth of Europe's third-biggest city (after Moscow and Istanbul) has been made possible by its public transit system.

An elevator whisks you to the top floor...and the year 1800, when horse-drawn vehicles ruled the road. London invented the notion of a public bus traveling a set route that anyone could board without a reservation. Next came steam-powered locomotives. Soon trains were speeding through tunnels beneath the city—the world's first underground Metro system (and today's Circle Line, begun c. 1865).

On the ground floor, horses and trains are quickly replaced by cars, taxis, red double-decker buses, streetcars, and 20th-century congestion.

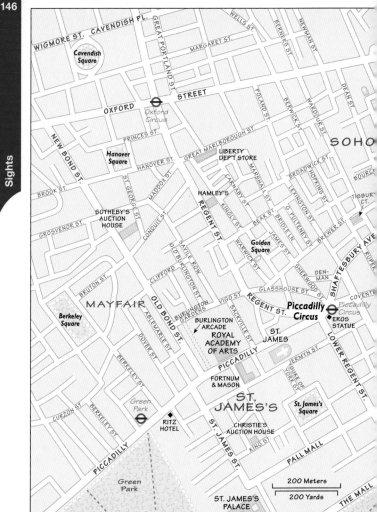

Sights

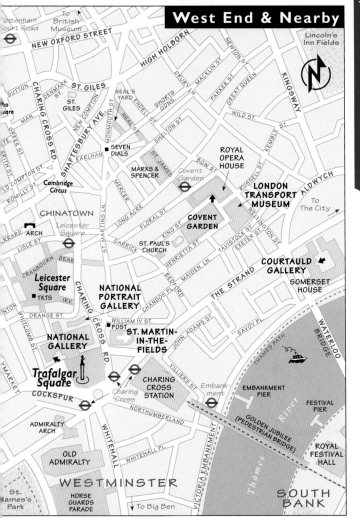

Sights

To Tottenham Court Road

To British Museum

NEW OXFORD STREET

HIGH HOLBORN

Lincoln's Inn Fields

SUTTON

DENMARK ST.

ST. GILES

CHARING CROSS RD.

ST. GILES

NEWTON ST.

Soho Square

MAN.

NEW COMPTON ST.

NEAL'S YARD

SHORTS GDNS.

DRURY LN.

MACKLIN ST.

PARKER ST.

GREAT QUEEN

KINGSWAY

GREEK ST.

FRITH ST.

ENDELL ST.

MONMOUTH ST.

NEAL ST.

SHELTON ST.

WILD ST.

OLD COMPTON ST.

SHAFTESBURY AVE.

SEVEN DIALS

EARLHAM

ST. JAMES'S

BOW ST.

ROYAL OPERA HOUSE

RUSSELL ST.

KEMBLE ST.

ROMILLY ST.

Cambridge Circus

MARKS & SPENCER

Covent Garden

LONDON TRANSPORT MUSEUM

ALDWYCH

To The City

CHINATOWN

GERRARD

ARCH

LISLE ST.

MERCER

LONG ACRE

FLORAL ST.

COVENT GARDEN

WELLINGTON ST.

Leicester Square

ST. MARTINS LN.

KING ST.

TAVISTOCK ST.

EXETER ST.

COURTAULD GALLERY

CRANBOURN

BEAR

GARRICK

ST. PAUL'S CHURCH

HENRIETTA ST.

BEDFORD

THE STRAND

SOMERSET HOUSE

Leicester Square

MAIDEN LN.

Leicester Square

TKTS

IRV.

NATIONAL PORTRAIT GALLERY

CHANDOS PL.

ORANGE ST.

CHARING CROSS RD.

WILLIAM IV ST.

POST

JOHN ADAMS ST.

SAVOY PL.

WATERLOO BRIDGE

NEWTON

WHITCOMB ST.

ST. MARTIN-IN-THE-FIELDS

NATIONAL GALLERY

Charing Cross

CHARING CROSS STATION

VILLIERS ST.

Embankment

THAMES PATH

EMBANKMENT PIER

Trafalgar Square

COCKSPUR

NORTHUMBERLAND

FESTIVAL PIER

HAYMARKET

ADMIRALTY ARCH

WHITEHALL

VICTORIA EMBANKMENT

GOLDEN JUBILEE (PEDESTRIAN BRIDGE)

Thames River

ROYAL FESTIVAL HALL

OLD ADMIRALTY

WHITEHALL PL.

St. James's Park

WESTMINSTER

HORSE GUARDS PARADE

To Big Ben

SOUTH BANK

How to deal with it? The rest of the museum has interactive exhibits that let you be part of the solution.

▶ *£13.50. Open Sat–Thu 10:00–18:00, Fri 11:00–18:00, last entry 45 minutes before closing. There's a pleasant upstairs café with Covent Garden view. Tube: Covent Garden. Switchboard tel. 020/7379-6344 or recorded info tel. 020/7565-7299, www.ltmuseum.co.uk.*

▲Courtauld Gallery

Just small enough that you could see it all in a single visit, this gallery of paintings makes for a pleasant experience. The collection spans the history of Western painting, from medieval altarpieces through Italian Renaissance to the 20th century. Its highlights are Impressionist and Post-Impressionist works, some of which you'll recognize.

Be sure to see Edouard Manet's *A Bar at the Folies-Bergère,* which places you in the center of a glittering dancehall, reflected in the bar mirror. Paul Cézanne foreshadows Cubism with a mountain landscape built out of cubes of paint.

There's also Vincent van Gogh's *Self-Portrait with Bandaged Ear,* painted in the aftermath of the insane episode where he threatened Gauguin with a knife, cut off a piece of his own ear, and gave it to a prostitute. Just released from the hospital, Van Gogh assesses himself. The self-portrait shows a calm man with an unflinching gaze. The slightly stained bandage over his ear is neither hidden in shame nor worn as a badge of honor. Doesn't this man realize that a year and a half later he'll take his own life?

▶ *£6, free Mon until 14:00. Open daily 10:00–18:00, last entry 30 minutes before closing, occasionally open Thu until 21:00. Located at Somerset House, along the Strand, a 15-minute walk from Trafalgar (Tube: Temple or Covent Garden). There's a downstairs cafeteria, plus other eateries around the complex. Shop tel. 020/7848-2579, recorded info tel. 020/7848-2526, www.courtauld.ac.uk.*

Buckingham Palace

Buckingham Palace has been the official residence of the monarch since 1837, when Queen Victoria moved in. Today, Queen Elizabeth II and Prince Philip live here most of the time (in the north wing), though they have other residences elsewhere. When the Queen's at home, the royal standard flies (a red, yellow, and blue flag); otherwise, the Union Jack flaps in the wind. The palace is a cozy little 830,000-square-foot pad, home to a concert

London for Early Birds and Night Owls

Most sightseeing in London is restricted to the hours between 10:00 and 18:00. Here are a few exceptions:

Sights Open Early
St. Paul's Cathedral: Mon–Sat at 8:30.
Shakespeare's Globe: Daily at 9:00.
Madame Tussauds: 9:00 or 9:30 depending on day and season.
Tower of London: Tue–Sat at 9:00.
Churchill War Rooms: Daily at 9:30.
Westminster Abbey: Mon–Sat at 9:30.
British Library: Mon–Sat at 9:30.

Sights Open Late
British Museum (most galleries): Fri until 20:30.
National Gallery: Fri until 21:00.
British Library: Tue until 20:00.
National Portrait Gallery: Thu–Fri until 21:00.
London Eye: Daily until 20:00, 21:00, or 21:30 depending on season.
Houses of Parliament (when in session): Mon–Tue until 22:30, Wed until 22:00, Thu until 19:00.
Madame Tussauds: Daily until 19:30 or 20:00, depending on day and season.
Vinopolis: Thu–Sat until 22:00.
Victoria and Albert Museum (selected galleries): Fri until 22:00.
Tate Modern: Fri–Sat until 22:00.
Tate Britain: First Fri of the month until 22:00.

hall (for command performances), ballrooms for state functions, and the large enclosed gardens in back. As the place where foreign leaders are received, it's become the symbol of the monarchy.

The area around the palace is mostly open space and gardens, with few tourist amenities. The wide boulevard called The Mall was built in 1911 as a ceremonial approach.

For tourists, there are several sights to see: the Changing of the Guard out front, the Queen's Gallery art collection in a palace annex, and the stables of the adjoining Royal Mews. The Palace's main interior is off-limits to tourists except for the State Rooms visits in August and September (Tube: Victoria, St. James's Park, or Green Park).

▲▲Changing of the Guard at Buckingham Palace

This is the spectacle every visitor to London has to see at least once: stone-faced, red-coated, bearskin-hatted guards changing posts with much fanfare, in an hour-long ceremony accompanied by a brass band. The main ceremony is right in front of the palace, but there's also camera-worthy action elsewhere—a second set of guards at nearby St. James's Palace (a half-mile northwest) and the fresh replacement guards at Wellington Barracks, 500 yards east of the palace (on Birdcage Walk). Get out your map and strategize.

It's 11:00 at Buckingham Palace, and the on-duty guards are ready to finish their shift. Shortly after, the tired guards at St. James's head down the Mall, joining forces with the recently relieved Horse Guard. Meanwhile, the replacement troops at Wellington Barracks, led by the band, also head for Buckingham Palace. By 11:45, they all converge on Buckingham Palace in a perfect storm of Red Coat pageantry. Everyone parades around, shouts, and the band plays a happy little concert. At noon, the tired guards head to Wellington Barracks and the fresh guards to St. James's Palace.

Most tourists just show up and get lost in the crowds. Pick one event and find a good unobstructed spot to see it. To see the actual changing in the Buckingham Palace forecourt (the main event, though it's rather dull), get there no later than 10:30 to get a place right next to the fence. But you could also find a spot at Wellington Barracks to watch the replacement guards mobilize (11:00–11:15), or St. James's Palace (11:00–11:15). Or stand along The Mall or Spur Road to watch them parade (11:15–11:30). Or watch them parade back along those same streets after the guard-change and most tourists have gone home (12:10).

The key is to visit one of the less-touristed areas (St. James's or Wellington Barracks), get right up front along the road or fence, or find some raised elevation to stand or sit on—a balustrade or a curb—so you can see over people's heads.

For the best overall view, stake out the high ground on the circular Victoria Memorial (come before 11:00 to get a place). From the Memorial, you have good views of the palace as well as the arriving and departing parades along The Mall and Spur Road. The whole area is usually a tourist crush. By 12:30, the army of tourists is "dismissed."

▶ *Free. The schedule varies day to day, so call or check the website for your exact visit. Generally, it's daily May–July at 11:30, every other day Aug–April, no ceremony in very wet weather. Tube: Victoria, St. James's*

Sights

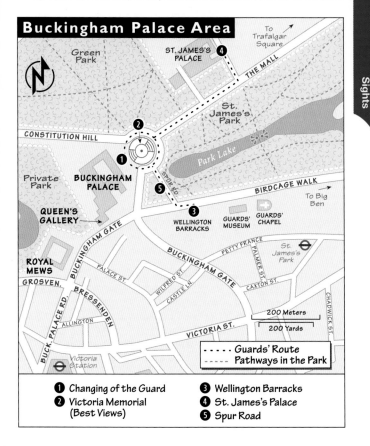

Buckingham Palace Area

- Green Park
- To Trafalgar Square
- ST. JAMES'S PALACE ④
- THE MALL
- CONSTITUTION HILL
- St. James's Park
- ❷
- ❶
- Park Lake
- Private Park
- BUCKINGHAM PALACE
- ❺
- BIRDCAGE WALK
- To Big Ben
- QUEEN'S GALLERY
- BUCKINGHAM GATE
- ❸
- WELLINGTON BARRACKS
- GUARDS' MUSEUM
- GUARDS' CHAPEL
- St. James's Park
- ROYAL MEWS
- GROSVEN.
- PALACE ST.
- WILFRED ST.
- CASTLE LN.
- BUCKINGHAM GATE
- PETTY FRANCE
- PALMER ST.
- CAXTON ST.
- CHADWICK ST.
- BRESSENDEN
- ALLINGTON
- BUCK. PALACE RD.
- VICTORIA ST.
- Victoria Station
- 200 Meters
- 200 Yards
- · · · · Guards' Route
- - - - - Pathways in the Park

❶ Changing of the Guard
❷ Victoria Memorial (Best Views)
❸ Wellington Barracks
❹ St. James's Palace
❺ Spur Road

Park, or Green Park. Or hop into a big black taxi and say, "Buck House, please." Tel. 020/7766-7300, www.changing-the-guard.com.

▲Queen's Gallery at Buckingham Palace

Queen Elizabeth's personal collection of art is on display in a wing adjoining the palace. You'll see just a handful of the Queen's huge 7,000-painting collection, which is considered the finest private art collection in the world. Small, thoughtfully presented, and always exquisite displays fill the five rooms open to the public. You'll also see temporary exhibits and a small room glittering with the Queen's personal jewelry. Compared to the crown jewels at the Tower, it may be Her Majesty's bottom drawer—but it's still a dazzling display. Men shouldn't miss the mahogany-trimmed urinals.

▸ *£7.50–9.25. Open daily 10:00–17:30, last entry one hour before closing, Tube: Victoria. Tel. 020/7766-7301, but Her Majesty rarely answers.*

Royal Mews

The Queen's working stables are just that. You'll see a few of the Queen's 30 horses, a fancy car, and a bunch of old carriages, finishing with the Gold State Coach (c. 1760, 4 tons, 4 mph). The excellent, included audioguide enlivens the visit.

▸ *£8.25. Open April–Oct daily 11:00–17:00, Nov–March Mon–Fri 10:00–16:00, closed Sat–Sun, last entry 45 minutes before closing. Guided tours on the hour. Located along Buckingham Palace Road, Tube: Victoria. Tel. 020/7766-7302.*

▲State Rooms at Buckingham Palace

In August and September, the Queen opens her lavish palace and throne room to the public—when she's out of town.

▸ *£18, includes audioguide. Open Aug–Sept only, daily 9:30–18:30, last admission 16:15. Tube: Victoria. It's crowded—come by 9:15 or book ahead at tel. 020/7766-7300 or www.royalcollection.org.uk.*

NORTH LONDON

▲▲▲British Museum
✪ See the British Museum Tour on page 75.

▲▲▲British Library
✪ See the British Library Tour on page 103.

▲Wallace Collection
Sir Richard Wallace's fine collection of 17th-century Dutch Masters, 18th-century French Rococo, medieval armor, and assorted aristocratic fancies fills a sumptuous mansion. Paintings of note include *The Laughing Cavalier* by Frans Hals (as you view the canvas from multiple angles, his smirking eyes follow you) and *The Swing* by Jean-Honoré Fragonard (featuring an oblivious husband, a lurking lover, and a swinging wife).

▶ *Free. Open daily 10:00–17:00. Tube: Bond Street. Tel. 020/7563-9500,*
www.wallacecollection.org.

▲Madame Tussauds Waxworks

This is gimmicky and expensive, but dang good...a hit with the kind of travelers who skip the British Museum.

The original Madame Tussaud did wax casts of heads lopped off during the French Revolution (such as Marie-Antoinette's). She took her show on the road and ended up in London in 1835. These days, it's all about squeezing Tom Cruise's bum, gambling with George Clooney, and partying with Beyoncé, Britney, and Brangelina. These wax dummies are eerily realistic. The place is one giant, crowded, chaotic photo-op, with everyone jockeying for position to pose next to some famous dummy. Count how many times you say "excuse me" after bumping into a wax figure.

Besides the line-up of A-list stars, you'll see sports heroes (Muhammad Ali, Tiger Woods), scientists (Einstein), artists (Van Gogh), writers (Shakespeare), and politicians (Barack Obama). You can pose with the Queen, Will, or Kate...or settle for Camilla. Other gimmicky attractions (haunted house, 3-D movie) please the kids. The line-up of dummies changes often, depending on who's hot.

▶ *£30. Open Mon–Fri 9:30–19:30, Sat–Sun 9:00–20:00, mid-July–Aug and school holidays daily 9:00–20:00, last entry two hours before closing. Located at Marylebone Road, Tube: Baker Street.*

To avoid the line, buy a Fast Track ticket or reserve online. Check the website for discounts on this pricey waxtravaganza. Toll tel. 0871-894-3000, www.madametussauds.com.

Sir John Soane's Museum

Architects and fans of eclectic knickknacks love this quirky place, as do fans of interior decor. Tour this furnished home on a bird-chirping square and see 19th-century chairs, lamps, and carpets, wood-paneled nooks and crannies, and stained-glass skylights. The townhouse is cluttered with Soane and his wife's collection of ancient relics, curios, and famous paintings, including Hogarth's series on *The Rake's Progress* (read the fun plot) and several excellent Canalettos. In 1833, just before his death, Soane established his house as a museum, stipulating that it be kept as nearly as possible in the state he left it. If he visited today, he'd be entirely satisfied. You'll leave wishing you'd known the man.

▶ *Free, but donations much appreciated. Open Tue–Sat 10:00–17:00, first Tue of the month also 18:00–21:00, last entry 30 minutes before closing. Long entry lines on Sat and first Tue. Located at 13 Lincoln's Inn Fields, a quarter-mile southeast of British Museum, Tube: Holborn. Tel. 020/7405-2107, www.soane.org.*

Pollock's Toy Museum

This small, rickety old house offers a time warp back to the age before batteries or computer chips. See 19th and 20th-century toys, games, and dolls (with good descriptions), including the toy invented when President Theodore Roosevelt refused to shoot a bear cub—the Teddy Bear.

▶ *£6, kids-£3. Generally open Mon–Sat 10:00–17:00, closed Sun, last entry 30 minutes before closing. Located at 1 Scala Street, Tube: Goodge Street. Tel. 020/7636-3452, www.pollockstoymuseum.com.*

Abbey Road—Beatles Photo-Op

London is surprisingly devoid of sights associated with the famous '60s rock band. For a photo-op, go to Abbey Road and walk the famous crosswalk pictured on the *Abbey Road* album cover. From the St. John's Wood Tube station, it's a five-minute walk west down Grove End Road to the intersection with Abbey Road. The Abbey Road recording studio where the Beatles often recorded is the low-key, white building to the right of Abbey House. It's still a working studio, so you can't go inside. Ponder the graffiti on the low wall outside, and...imagine. To recreate the famous cover photo, shoot the crosswalk from the roundabout as you face north up Abbey Road. Shoes are optional.

THE CITY

In Shakespeare's day, London consisted of a one-square-mile area surrounding St. Paul's. Today, that square mile—the neighborhood known as "The City"—is still the financial heart of London, densely packed with history and bustling with business.

The City stretches from Temple Church (near Blackfriars Bridge) to the Tower of London. Its spine is a single east-west street that changes names—the Strand becomes Fleet Street, which becomes Cannon Street.

This was the London of the ancient Romans, William the Conqueror, Henry VIII, Shakespeare, and Elizabeth I. But The City has been stripped of its history by the Great Fire (1666), the WWII Blitz (1940–1941), and modern economic realities.

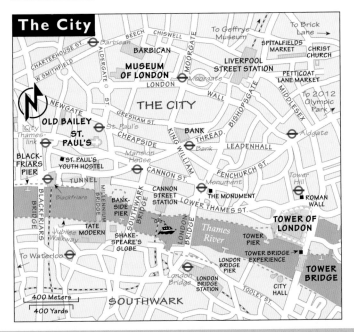

Cockney Rhyming Slang

The East End (specifically, the area around the Church of St. Mary-le-Bow) is known as the traditional home of the Cockneys. This colorful, working-class group spoke in a colorful pastiche that was the opposite of the Queen's English...think Audrey Hepburn as Eliza Doolittle in *My Fair Lady*, Dick van Dyke as the chimneysweep in *Mary Poppins,* or Don Cheadle in *Ocean's Eleven*.

One colorful Cockney invention that survives today is their unique rhyming slang. They replace an everyday word with a nonsensical phrase that rhymes with it. Instead of "beers," they say "Britney Spears," so they might say: "Let's head to the pub for some Britneys."

Sights

Today, it's a neighborhood of modern bank buildings and retail stores. Only about 7,000 people actually live here, but on work days it's packed with hundreds of thousands of commuting bankers, legal assistants, and coffee-shop baristas. By day, The City is a hive of business activity. At night and on weekends, it's a ghost town.

▲▲▲St. Paul's Cathedral
✪ See St. Paul's Tour on page 115.

▲Old Bailey
England's most infamous criminals—from the king-killers of the Civil War to the radically religious William Penn, from the "criminally homosexual" Oscar Wilde to the Yorkshire Ripper—were tried here, in Britain's highest criminal court. Today, they still dole out justice the old-fashioned way. Bewigged barristers argue before stern judges while the accused sits in the dock. It's open to the public when court is in session.

▶ *Free. Open generally Mon–Fri 9:45–13:00 & 14:00–16:00. Tight security—check bags at Capable Travel Agency, just down the street at Old Bailey 4—£5/bag, £1 per phone or camera. Located on Old Bailey Street, follow signs to visitor's entrance, Tube: St. Paul's. Tel. 020/7248-3277.*

Harry Potter's London

Harry Potter's story is set in a magical Britain, and most of the places mentioned in the books are fictional, but you can visit many real (if un-magical) film locations.

Harry's story begins in suburban London, in the fictional town of Little Whinging, shot in the town of **Bracknell** (pop. 50,000, 10 miles west of Heathrow), at #4 Privet Drive. Harry first realizes his wizard powers when talking with a boa constrictor, filmed at the **London Zoo's Reptile House** in Regent's Park (Tube: Great Portland Street).

Big Ben and **Parliament,** along the Thames, welcome Harry to the modern city inhabited by non-magical Muggles. Harry shops for Hogwarts school supplies along Charing Cross Road, actually filmed in glass-roofed **Leadenhall Market** (Tube: Bank) along Bull's Head Passage. Goblin-run Gringotts Wizarding Bank was filmed in the chandeliered entryway of **Australia House** (Tube: Temple).

Harry catches the train to Hogwarts at **King's Cross/St. Pancras Station.** Harry departs from magical **platform 9¾** (where the station has placed a sign and disappearing luggage cart near real platform 9 in the western departures concourse).

In *the Prisoner of Azkaban* film, Harry careens through London's lamp-lit streets on a three-decker bus that dumps him off on rough-looking Stoney Street at the southeast edge of **Borough Street Market** (Tube: London Bridge). In *the Half-Blood Prince* film, the **Millennium Bridge** collapses into the Thames.

For the *Deathly Hallows* film, the real government offices of **Whitehall** serve as the location for the Ministry of Magic.

Other London settings, like Diagon Alley, only exist at **Leavesden Film Studios** (20 miles north of London), where most of the films' interiors were shot. Leavesden recently opened its doors to Harry Potter pilgrims, who come to see many of the original sets and props on the Warner Bros. Studio Tour (£28, kids ages 5 to 15-£21, family ticket for 2 adults and 2 kids-£83, £5 extra for audio/videoguide, tours depart daily 10:00-18:00, tel. 0845-084-0900, www.wbstudiotour.co.uk).

Finally, cinema buffs can visit **Leicester Square** (Tube: Leicester Square), where Daniel Radcliffe and other stars have strolled past paparazzi and down red carpets to attend the movies' premieres.

▲Museum of London

Trace the fascinating story of London's distinguished citizens, from Neanderthals to Romans to Elizabethans to Victorians to Mods to today. The museum's displays are chronological, spacious, and informative without being overwhelming. Scale models and costumes help you visualize everyday life in the city at different periods. There are enough whiz-bang multimedia displays (including the Plague and the Great Fire) to spice up otherwise humdrum artifacts. This regular stop for the local school kids gives the best overview of London history in town.

▶ *Free, daily 10:00–18:00, last entry 30 minutes before closing, see the day's events board for special talks and tours, on London Wall at Aldersgate Street, Tube: Barbican or St. Paul's plus a five-minute walk. Tel. 020/7001-9844, www.museumoflondon.org.uk.*

"The Monument" to the Great Fire

The 202-foot column known as "The Monument," built by Christopher Wren, commemorates the Great Fire that transformed London.

At 2:00 in the morning of September 2, 1666, a small fire broke out in a baker's oven in nearby Pudding Lane. Supposedly, if you tipped the Monument over (to the east), its top would fall on the exact spot. Fanned by hot, blustery weather, the fire swept westward, leaping from house to house. It engulfed the mostly wooden city, devouring Old St. Paul's, and continuing to Temple Church, until The City was a square mile of flame. In four days, 80 percent of London was incinerated, including 13,000 houses and 89 churches. The good news? Incredibly, only nine people died, the fire cleansed a plague-infested city, and Christopher Wren was around to rebuild London's skyline.

You can climb the Monument's 311 steps for a view that's still pretty monumental.

▶ *£3, daily 9:30–17:30, last entry at 17:00. Located at the northeast end of London Bridge, Tube: Monument. Tel. 020/7626-2717, www.the monument.info.*

▲▲▲Tower of London

✪ See the Tower of London Tour on page 127.

Tower Bridge

The iconic Tower Bridge—often mistakenly called London Bridge—was

2012 London Olympics

From July 27 to August 12, 2012, all eyes were on London as it hosted athletes from 205 nations in the 30th Olympiad. Festivities centered around Olympic Park, filling the Lea Valley, about seven miles northeast of downtown London. Lea Valley used to be the site of derelict factories, mountains of discarded tires, and Europe's biggest refrigerator dump. But now, this area glistens with gardens, greenery, and state-of-the-art construction.

London is the first city to host the modern games three times—first in 1908, then in 1948 (the first post-World-War-II Olympics, known as the "Austerity Games"). The city won the 2012 bid for its grand and green vision, including a promise to permanently improve the least desirable part of the city. The site's connection to the broader world was extraordinary: It takes less than three hours to go from Paris to Olympic Park (the Eurostar zips to St. Pancras International Station in downtown London, which connects via a seven-minute bullet train to Stratford International Station).

built in 1894 as a hydraulically powered drawbridge to accommodate the growing East End. You can tour the bridge and its workings at the Tower Bridge Experience.

► £7, daily 10:00–18:00 in summer, 9:30–17:30 in winter, last entry 30 minutes before closing. Tube: Tower Hill. Tel. 020/7403-3761, www.tower bridge.org.uk.

Olympic Park

Olympic Park was the heart of the 2012 Summer Games, home to the 80,000-seat Olympic Stadium (used for opening and closing ceremonies), the Olympic Village, where the athletes stayed, and a giant climbable sculpture called the Orbit. The 12,000-seat basketball arena was designed to be completely dismantled when the games were over. The Aquatics Centre, with its swooping wave-like roofline, is recognizable as the architectural "face" of the games.

After the games ended, the park was closed, as the city worked to convert many of the facilities for long-term use, such as housing. Most of it is off-limits to visitors until spring of 2014, though the northern part of the park may be open in summer of 2013. In the meantime, much of the park and its structures are visible from the View Tube (free, daily 9:00–17:00, 25 minutes from downtown London, connect by Tube to DLR, stop: Pudding Mill Lane, www.theviewtube.co.uk).

THE SOUTH BANK

South of the Thames is a thriving area tied together by a riverside pedestrian path called the Jubilee Walkway. Stretching from the London Eye to London Bridge, it offers grand views of the city skyline across the river. On a sunny day, this is the place to see London out strolling.

The area hosts major sights—Shakespeare's Globe, the Tate Modern—plus some tacky ones, all spiced with pleasant pubs, theatres, and cafes. Helpful Tube stops are Warterloo, Southwark, and London Bridge.

▲▲London Eye

The giant Ferris wheel, towering above London opposite Big Ben, is London's answer to the Eiffel Tower. While the experience is memorable, London doesn't have much of a skyline to see, and the price is borderline outrageous.

Twenty-five people ride in each of its 32 air-conditioned capsules for the 30-minute rotation (you go around only once). From the top of this 443-foot-high wheel—the highest public viewpoint in the city, with 25 miles' visibility on the rare clear day—even Big Ben looks small. While it was built to celebrate the new millennium, the Eye's original five-year lease has been extended, and it's becoming a permanent fixture of the London skyline.

Your ticket also includes a bombastic-but-fun four-minute, 3-D movie. By the Eye there's a cotton-candy tourist zone of kitschy, kid-friendly attractions, as well as Thames cruise boats.

▶ £19, various combo-tickets available with other attractions. Open daily July–Aug 10:00–21:30, April–June 10:00–21:00, Sept–March 10:00–20:00, these are last-ascent times, closed Dec 25 and a few days in Jan. Tube: Waterloo or Westminster.

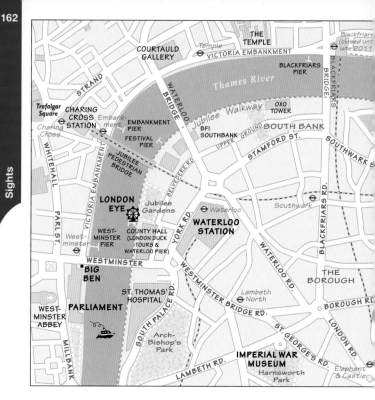

Expect 30-minute waits to buy tickets plus 30–45-minute waits to board especially on weekends between 11:00 and 17:00, and every day July–Aug. A £10 Fast Track supplement lets you walk straight on. Avoid the ticket-buying part of the wait by booking online (10 percent discount) or telephone. Tel. 0870-500-0600, www.londoneye.com.

▲▲Imperial War Museum

This impressive museum covers the wars of the last century. Most of the displays are low-tech—dummies in uniforms, weapons, newspaper

The South Bank

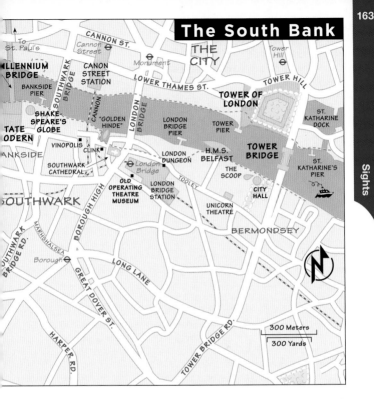

clippings, ordinary objects from daily life—but the explanations are excellent and there are enough multimedia exhibits to keep it lively.

Start with World War I, where "The Trench Experience" lets you walk through a dark, chaotic, smelly bunker. The World War II rooms are augmented by the Blitz Experience, a walk-through simulator that assaults the senses with the noise and intensity of a Nazi air raid.

You'll see vintage planes, tanks, submarines, and a 50-foot V-2 rocket, the kind Hitler rained down on London. The section on the "Secret War" peeks into the intrigues of espionage. The Holocaust exhibit is one of the best on the subject anywhere. The displays continue through the Cold War, the Cuban Missile Crisis, the Troubles in Northern Ireland, the wars in Iraq, and terrorism.

Rather than glorify war, the museum shines a light on the 100 million deaths of the 20th century—the tragic consequence of one of humankind's most persistent traits.

▸ *Free, but optional temporary exhibits extra. Open daily 10:00–18:00. Tube: Lambeth North. Tel. 020/7416-5000, www.iwm.org.uk.*

▲▲Tate Modern

Dedicated in the spring of 2000, the striking museum across the river from St. Paul's opened the new century with art from the previous one. Its powerhouse collection of Monet, Matisse, Dalí, Picasso, Warhol, and much more is displayed in a converted powerhouse. A new annex is opening next door to show more art.

The permanent collection is on the third and fifth floors. Paintings are arranged according to theme, not chronologically or by artist. Paintings by Picasso, for example, are scattered all over the building. Don't just come to see the Old Masters of modernism. Push your mental envelope with more recent works by Pollock, Miró, Bacon, Picabia, Beuys, Twombly, and others.

Of equal interest are the many temporary exhibits featuring cutting-edge art. Each year, the main hall features a different monumental installation by a prominent artist—always one of the highlights of the art world.

▸ *Free but £4 donations appreciated, fee for optional special exhibitions. Open daily 10:00–18:00, Fri–Sat until 22:00—good times to visit. Free guided tours several times a day. View restaurant on top floor. Located across the Millennium Bridge from St. Paul's. Tube: Southwark, London Bridge, or Mansion House. Tel. 020/7887-8888, www.tate.org.uk.*

▲Millennium Bridge

The pedestrian bridge linking St. Paul's Cathedral and the Tate Modern opened in the year 2000. Almost immediately, the $25 million "bridge to the next millennium" started wobbling dangerously (insert your own ironic joke here). Now stabilized, it's won praise for Sir Norman Foster's sleek minimalist design—370 yards long, four yards wide, of stainless steel with teak planks. The clever aerodynamic handrails deflect wind over the heads of pedestrians.

▲▲Shakespeare's Globe

> *All the world's a stage,*
> *And all the men and women merely players.*
> *They have their exits and their entrances,*
> *And one man, in his time, plays many parts.*
> —As You Like It

In 1599, 35-year-old William Shakespeare and his theatre company opened the 3,000-seat Globe Theatre, by far the largest of its day. The Globe premiered Shakespeare's greatest works—*Hamlet, Othello, King Lear, Macbeth*—in open-air summer afternoon performances.

In 1612, during a performance of *Henry VIII*, a stage cannon sparked a fire. Within an hour, the wood-and-thatch building had burned completely to the ground. In 1997, this replica was built—round, half-timbered, and thatched—located a block from the original site. It's a working theater, hosting plays virtually every day May-September. In 2014, the new Jacobean Theatre next door will allow indoor performances. Productions range from Shakespeare plays in period costumes to modern interpretations of his works and some works by other playwrights. (See www.shakespearesglobe.com for schedule and ticket info.)

Like the old Globe, the new one has an open-air roof, standing room by the stage, and no curtain. It's also more modern—with female actors, lights for night performances, a concrete floor, and fire-resistant materials. Today's Globe accommodates 800 seated and 600 standing versus Shakespeare's 2,200 seated and 1,000 groundlings.

You can tour the theatre and "Globe Exhibition" museum. The museum has Elizabethan-era costumes, scale models, and some early folios—the first publications of Shakespeare's plays. Next, a guide leads you into the theater to see the stage and the different seating areas for the different classes of people. It's not a backstage tour—you don't see dressing rooms or sit in on rehearsals—but the guides are energetic and theatrical, bringing the Elizabethan period to life.

▶ *£13.50 includes museum and 40-minute tour. Open daily 9:00–17:00, tours start every 15–30 minutes. During theatre season (May–Sept), Globe tours are offered mornings only, though you can visit the nearby (and less interesting) Rose Theatre in the afternoon. The theatre complex also has a box office and three eateries, from fancy to* *take-out. Located near the Tate Modern smokestack, Tube: Mansion House or London Bridge. Tel. 020/7902-1400 or 020/7902-1500, www .shakespearesglobe.com.*

▲Southwark

The area between the Tate Modern and London Bridge is known as Southwark (SUTH-uck). In Shakespeare's day, this was the rowdy neighborhood where Londoners went for a night of theater, bear-and-dog fights, brothels, and rollicking pubs. Today it's been gentrified, and within a few blocks, you'll find several interesting (and some tacky) sights.

Vinopolis: City of Wine: This huge wine museum offers a light yet earnest history of wine to accompany your sips of various mediocre reds and whites, ports, and champagnes.

▶ *Options range from £20 to £65, including about five wine tastes and an audioguide. Open Thu–Fri 14:00–22:00, Sat 12:00–22:00, Sun 12:00–18:00, last entry 2.5 hours before closing. Book ahead for crowded Fri–Sat nights. Located at 1 Bank End, Tube: London Bridge. Tel. 020/7940-3000, www.vinopolis.co.uk.*

The Clink Prison Museum: This was, until 1780, where law-abiding citizens threw Southwark troublemakers. Today, it's a low-tech, tacky torture museum filling grotty old rooms with papier-mâché gore.

▶ *Overpriced at £5. Open July–Sept daily 10:00–21:00; Oct–June Mon–Fri 10:00–18:00, Sat–Sun until 19:30. Located at 1 Clink Street, Tube: London Bridge. Tel. 020/7403-0900, www.clink.co.uk.*

Golden Hinde Replica: As we all learned in school, "Sir Francis Drake circumcised the globe with a hundred-foot clipper." Or something like that... This is a full-size, working replica of that 16th-century warship in which Drake circumnavigated the globe (1577–1580), earning him the reputation as history's most successful pirate. When he returned, a grateful Queen Elizabeth knighted Drake on the main deck and kissed him on his *Golden Hinde*.

▶ *£6 to go inside (not worth it). Open daily 10:00–17:30. Tube: London Bridge. Tel. 020/7403-0123, www.goldenhinde.com.*

Southwark Cathedral: While made a cathedral only in 1905, it's been the neighborhood church since the 13th century. Highlights include a Shakespeare memorial (right wall), a chapel to university-founding John Harvard (left wall), and daily evensong services (weekdays at 17:30, Sat at 16:00, Sun at 15:00).

> *Free but suggested donation. Open daily 8:00–18:00. Tube: London Bridge. Tel. 020/7367-6700, http://cathedral.southwark.anglican.org.*

Borough Market: For a thousand years, there's been a produce market here. These days, under a Victorian arcade, vendors sell products to wholesalers weekday mornings and to the general public on Thursday and Friday afternoons and all day Saturday. It's become a trendy spot for people-watching and cafe-sitting.

> *Located next to Southwark Cathedral, Tube: London Bridge.*

▲Old Operating Theatre Museum and Herb Garret

Climb a tight and creaky staircase to find a garret used to dry medicinal herbs, crude Victorian surgical instruments reminiscent of Black & Decker, and a special look at anesthetics—ether, chloroform, or three pints of ale.

Then you stumble upon Britain's oldest operating theater—a semi-circular room accommodating 150 spectators—where doctors sawed off limbs while med students observed. The wood still bears bloodstains. Nearly one in three patients died. There was a fine line between Victorian-era surgeons and Jack the Ripper.

> *£6, cash only. Open daily 10:30–16:45. At 9a St. Thomas Street, Tube: London Bridge. Tel. 020/7188-2679, www.thegarret.org.uk.*

The Shard

Rocketing dramatically 1,020 feet above the south end of the London Bridge, this brand-new addition to London's skyline is the tallest building in all of Europe (for now). The tip houses a 15-story stack of (enclosed) observation platforms.

> *£30, daily 9:00–22:00, last entry at 20:30, save £5 and skip lines by booking online at least 24 hours ahead, tel. 0844-499-7111, www.the -shard.com.*

City Hall

The glassy, egg-shaped building near the south end of Tower Bridge is London's City Hall, which houses the office of London's mayor—the flamboyant, conservative former journalist Boris Johnson. You can observe the chambers at work when they are in session. Next to City Hall is the outdoor amphi¬theater called The Scoop.

> *Free and open to visitors Mon–Thu 8:30–18:00, Fri 8:30–17:30, closed Sat–Sun. Tube: London Bridge. Tel. 020/7983-4000.*

Sights

WEST LONDON

▲▲Tate Britain

One of Europe's great art houses, the recently-renovated Tate Britain specializes in British painting from the 16th century through modern times. This is people's art, with realistic paintings rooted in the people, landscape, and stories of the British Isles.

You'll see Hogarth's sketches of gritty London life, Gainsborough's twinkle-toe ladies, Blake's glowing angels, Constable's clouds, the swooning realism of the Pre-Raphaelites, and room after room of Turner's proto-Impressionist tempests. In the modern art wing, there are Francis Bacon's screaming nightmares, Henry Moore statues, and the camera-eye portraits of Hockney and Freud.

Even if these names are new to you, don't worry. You'll likely see a few "famous" works you didn't know were British and exit the Tate Britain with at least one new favorite artist.

▶ *Free, £4 donation requested, optional temporary exhibits extra. Open daily 10:00–18:00, select Fri until 22:00 (check online), last entry to special exhibits 45 minutes before closing. Free tours offered daily. Café and restaurant. Located at Tube: Pimlico. Switchboard tel. 020/7887-8888, www.tate.org.uk.*

▲Apsley House (Wellington Museum)

Having beaten Napoleon at Waterloo, Arthur Wellesley, the First Duke of Wellington, was the most famous man in Europe. He was given a huge fortune with which he purchased London's ultimate address, #1 London. His refurbished mansion offers a nice interior, a handful of world-class paintings, and a glimpse at the life of the great soldier and two-time prime minister.

An 11-foot statue of Napoleon, clad only in a fig leaf, greets you. Napoleon had commissioned the statue, but after Napoleon's defeat, Wellington acquired it as a war trophy. The two great men were polar opposites—Napoleon the daring general and champion of revolution, Wellington the play-it-safe strategist and conservative politician—but they're forever linked in history.

You'll see precious objects given by the crowned heads of Europe, who were eternally grateful to Wellington for saving their necks from the

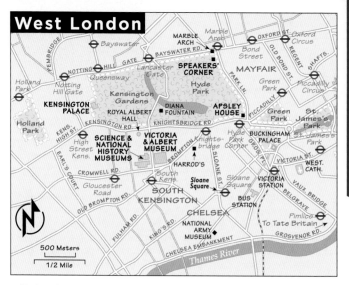

guillotine. Among the wall-to-wall paintings are Van Dyck's *Charles I on Horseback* and works by Velázquez, Jan Steen, and Goya.

There's also a pair of Wellington's boots, which the duke popularized—Brits today still call rubber boots "wellies."

▶ £6.70, free on June 18—Waterloo Day. Open April–Oct Wed–Sun 11:00–17:00, closed Mon–Tue; Nov–March Sat–Sun 10:00–16:00, closed Mon–Fri, no photos. Tube: Hyde Park Corner. Tel. 020/7499-5676, www.english-heritage.org.uk.

▲Hyde Park and Speakers' Corner

London's "Central Park," originally Henry VIII's hunting grounds, has more than 600 acres of lush greenery. There's the huge manmade Serpentine Lake, the royal Kensington Palace, the ornate Albert Memorial across from the Royal Albert Hall, and (nearby) the Princess Diana Memorial Fountain. The western half of the park is known as Kensington Gardens.

On Sundays, from just after noon until early evening, Speakers' Corner offers soapbox oratory at its best (northeast corner of the park, Tube: Marble Arch). Characters climb their stepladders, wave their flags, pound emphatically on their sandwich boards, and share what they are convinced is their wisdom. Regulars have resident hecklers who know their lines and are always ready with a verbal jab or barb. "The grass roots of democracy" originated when the gallows stood here and the criminal was allowed to say just about anything he wanted to before he swung. I dare you to raise your voice and gather a crowd—it's easy to do.

Sights

▲▲▲Victoria and Albert Museum

The world's top collection of decorative arts (vases, stained glass, fine furniture, clothing, jewelry, carpets, and more) is an eclectic and surprisingly interesting assortment. Throw in historical artifacts, a few masterpieces of painting and sculpture, and a bed that sleeps seven, and you have a museum built for browsing.

Here's just a sample: One of Leonardo da Vinci's notebooks, underwear through the ages, a Chihuly chandelier, a life-size *David* with detachable fig leaf, Henry VIII's quill pen, and Mick Jagger's sequined jumpsuit. From the worlds of Islam and India, there are stunning carpets, the ring of the man who built the Taj Mahal, and a mechanical tiger that eats Brits. Best of all, the objects are all quite beautiful. You could spend days in the place. Pick up a museum map and wander at will.

► *Free, £5 donation requested, fees for special exhibits. Open daily 10:00–17:45, some galleries open Fri until 22:00. Free tours several times daily. Tube: South Kensington, from the Tube station a long tunnel leads directly to museum. Tel. 020/7942-2000, www.vam.ac.uk.*

▲▲Natural History Museum

Across the street from Victoria and Albert, this mammoth museum contains 50 million specimens of earth's treasures—living things in one half, inanimate rocks and geology in the other. In the main hall, above a big dinosaur skeleton and under a massive slice of sequoia tree, Charles Darwin sits as if upon a throne overseeing it all.

Kids and non-science majors love the place. Well-explained and interactive exhibits cover dinosaurs, human evolution, creepy-crawlies, volcanoes, and more. Special tours and events are offered almost daily. Don't miss the meteorite from Mars and the Aurora Pyramid of Hope, displaying 296 diamonds showing their full range of natural colors. Pop into the wild collection of dinosaurs if only to hear English children exclaim, "Oh my goodness!"

▶ *Free, fees for special exhibits. Open daily 10:00–17:50, until 22:30 last Fri of month. A long tunnel leads directly from South Kensington Tube station to the museum. Tel. 020/7942-5011, www.nhm.ac.uk.*

▲Science Museum

Next door to the Natural History Museum, this sprawling wonderland for curious minds is kid-perfect, with themes such as measuring time, exploring space, and the evolution of modern medicine. It offers hands-on fun, from moonwalks to deep-sea exploration, with trendy technology, always interesting temporary exhibits, and an IMAX theater (£8).

▶ *Free, open daily 10:00–18:00, until 19:00 during school holidays. Tube: South Kensington. Tel. 0870-870-4868, www.sciencemuseum.org.uk.*

▲▲Kensington Palace

For nearly 150 years (1689-1837), Kensington was the royal residence, before Buckingham Palace became the official home of the monarch. Sitting primly on its pleasant parkside grounds, the palace is immaculately restored and creatively presented, with exhibits designed to appeal to adults and kids alike. It gives a fun glimpse into the lives of several important residents, especially Queen Victoria, who was born and raised here. It's strange to think that, in this city that was so shaped by Victoria, this is London's first and only museum that's truly about Victoria.

After Queen Victoria moved the monarchy to Buckingham Palace, lesser royals bedded down at Kensington. Princess Diana (1996-1997) lived here both during and after her marriage to Prince Charles. More recently, Will and Kate moved into a thoroughly renovated Apartment 1A (the southern flank of the palace complex, with four stories and 20 rooms). And Prince Harry lives in their old digs, a "cottage" on the other side of the main building. However—as many disappointed visitors discover—none of these more recent apartments are open to the public.

The exhibit is divided into three routes: the Queen's State Apartments (highly conceptual exhibits focusing on the later Stuart dynasty); the King's State Apartments (the grandest spaces, from Hanoverian times); and "Victoria Revealed" (the most worthwhile of the three).

▶ *£16.50. Open daily 10:00–18:00, until 17:00 in winter, last entry one hour before closing. It's a 10-minute hike through Kensington Gardens from either Queensway or High Street Kensington Tube station. Toll tel. 0870-751-5170 or 0844-482-7777, www.hrp.org.uk.*

GREATER LONDON

London's excellent public transit makes a number of outlying sights accessible. I've highlighted four of my favorites. For three of the following sights, consider Thames boat cruises as a scenic alternative to the train or Tube.

▲▲Kew Gardens

For a fine riverside park and a palatial greenhouse jungle to swing through, take the Tube or the boat to every botanist's favorite escape, Kew Gardens. Garden lovers could spend days here. Wander across 300 acres, among 33,000 different types of plants, representing the botanical diversity of our planet.

For a fragrant one-hour visit, concentrate on three buildings. The Palm House is a humid Victorian world of iron, glass, and tropical plants built in 1844. The Waterlily House has sights Monet would swim for. The Princess of Wales Conservatory is a modern greenhouse with many different climate zones growing countless cacti, bug-munching carnivorous plants, and more. The Rhizotron and Xstrata Treetop Walkway, a 200-yard-long steel footbridge—puts you high in the canopy 60 feet above the ground.

End your visit with a sun-dappled lunch or afternoon tea at the Orangery.

▶ £14. Open April–Aug Mon–Fri 9:30–18:30, Sat–Sun 9:30–19:30, closes earlier Sept–March. Galleries and conservatories close at 17:30 in high season, earlier off-season.

Getting There: The Kew Gardens Tube station is two blocks from the main entrance. Boats run April–Oct from Westminster Pier—✪ see page 230. Switchboard tel. 020/8332-5000, recorded info tel. 020/8332-5655, www.kew.org.

▲▲Greenwich

Just downstream from London, Greenwich is the destination for all things salty, including the *Cutty Sark* clipper ship, the area's premier attraction (it's a good idea to reserve a ticket in advance and plan your day around your entry time). At the Royal Observatory, visitors pose for a photo-op along the prime meridian (0° longitude), straddling two hemispheres, while

Sights

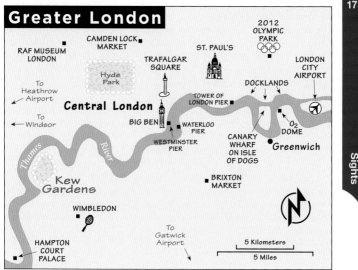

Greater London

RAF MUSEUM LONDON

CAMDEN LOCK MARKET

ST. PAUL'S

2012 OLYMPIC PARK

LONDON CITY AIRPORT

TRAFALGAR SQUARE

Hyde Park

To Heathrow Airport

DOCKLANDS

Central London

TOWER OF LONDON PIER

To Windsor

BIG BEN

WATERLOO PIER

CANARY WHARF ON ISLE OF DOGS

O₂ DOME

WESTMINSTER PIER

Greenwich

Thames River

BRIXTON MARKET

Kew Gardens

WIMBLEDON

To Gatwick Airport

5 Kilometers

5 Miles

HAMPTON COURT PALACE

Sights

they set their watches to coordinate to Greenwich Mean Time, measured from here. Thanks to this time standard (and to seaworthy clocks that could be taken aboard ships), sailors could finally plot their east-west (longitudinal) location.

The National Maritime Museum holds everything from a *Titanic* passenger's pocket watch to the uniform Admiral Nelson wore when he was killed at Trafalgar (find the bullet hole). The town of Greenwich is a pleasant, manageable place for a riverside stroll, enjoying stunning Baroque architecture and open-air markets. Finish your stroll with lunch at the Trafalgar Tavern, a pub Charles Dickens wrote about. Ahoy!

▶ Most sights are open daily and many are free, but the town's popular market is closed Monday.

Getting There: Boats depart from the piers at Westminster, Waterloo, and the Tower of London (2/hour, 1–1.25 hours). By train, catch the DLR from Bank Tube station to Cutty Sark (20 minutes, 5/hour, covered by any Tube pass).

▲Hampton Court Palace

Fifteen miles up the Thames from downtown (a £20 taxi ride from Kew Gardens), and worth ▲▲ for palace aficionados, is the 500-year-old palace of Henry VIII. The stately Tudor palace overlooking the Thames was also home to Elizabeth I and Charles I. Visitors can see impressive Tudor rooms, including the King's apartments and a Great Hall with a magnificent hammer-beam ceiling. The industrial-strength Tudor kitchen was capable of keeping 600 schmoozing courtiers thoroughly fed. The sculpted garden features a rare Tudor tennis court and a popular maze. The palace tries hard to please, but it doesn't quite sparkle.

▸ *£17, online discounts. Open daily April–Oct 10:00–18:00, Nov–March 10:00–16:30, last entry one hour before closing, café.*

Getting There: The train (2/hour, 35 minutes) from London's Waterloo Station drops you across the river from the palace (just walk across the bridge). The boat from Westminster Pier (✪ see page 230) is a relaxing and scenic three- to four-hour cruise past two locks and a fun new/old riverside mix.

Toll tel. 0844-482-7777, www.hrp.org.uk.

▲Windsor

Queen Elizabeth II's preferred residence is Windsor Castle, set in the compact, pedestrian-friendly town of Windsor (pop. 30,000). Here you can see a low-key Changing of the Guard, the castle's lavish staterooms (perhaps Britain's best), an impressive royal art collection, some royal tombs, and Queen Mary's Dollhouse—a 1:12 scale palace in miniature.

▸ *Castle costs £17. To skip lines, purchase tickets in advance online or at Buckingham Palace ticket office, then go in through fast entry door. Open daily March–Oct 9:45–17:15, Nov–Feb 9:45–16:15, last entry 1.25 hours before closing, may close for special events—call first, tel. 020/7766-7304, www.royalcollection.org.uk.*

Getting There: Trains run from both Paddington and Waterloo Stations (35–60 min, 2/hour, £9–15 round trip), dropping you a 5-minute walk from the castle.

Sleeping

London hotels are expensive. I prefer places that are clean, central, friendly, quiet, offer good value, and are small enough to have a hands-on owner and stable staff. Four of these six virtues means it's a keeper. Most of all, I emphasize location—in seven safe, pleasant neighborhoods convenient to sightseeing.

The **Victoria Station** neighborhood (near Big Ben and Buckingham Palace) is central as can be. The area is surprisingly safe, tidy, and full of decent eateries, and most hotels are a five-minute walk from Tube, bus, and train stations. **South Kensington** (west of Big Ben) is quiet, classy, and upscale, conveniently located on the Tube Circle Line. Residential **Notting Hill** (west of Hyde Park) is farther from the action, but it's also trendy and popular with the young international set. **Paddington Station** (north of Hyde Park) is less charming but has all the travelers' amenities and convenient transportation connections.

Sleeping

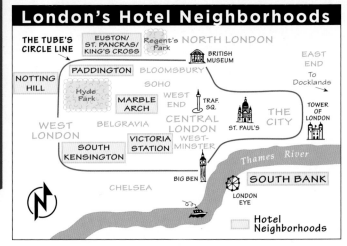

London's Hotel Neighborhoods

THE TUBE'S CIRCLE LINE

EUSTON/ ST. PANCRAS/ KING'S CROSS

Regent's Park

NORTH LONDON

BRITISH MUSEUM

EAST END

To Docklands

NOTTING HILL

PADDINGTON

BLOOMSBURY

SOHO

Hyde Park

MARBLE ARCH

WEST END

TRAF. SQ.

WEST LONDON

BELGRAVIA

CENTRAL LONDON

ST. PAUL'S

THE CITY

TOWER OF LONDON

SOUTH KENSINGTON

VICTORIA STATION

WEST-MINSTER

BIG BEN

Thames River

CHELSEA

LONDON EYE

SOUTH BANK

Hotel Neighborhoods

You'll find convenient (if less charming) places near **Euston, St. Pancras, and King's Cross Stations**. The centrally located neighborhood **north of Marble Arch** is classy and close to Oxford Street shopping. Finally, for those wanting to stay south of the Thames near Shakespeare's Globe, there's the **South Bank.**

Double rooms listed in this book average around £100 (including a private bathroom). They range from around £60 (safe but cramped, with a bathroom down the hall) to £150 or more (spacious, elegant places with all the modern conveniences). Those on a tight budget may have to choose between a modern-but-soulless place, or family-run friendliness in a cracked-plaster building.

A typical £100 double room will be small and old-fashioned by American standards. It will have one double bed or two twins. There's a bathroom in the room with a toilet, sink, and shower. The room has a telephone, a TV, and usually a plug-in kettle with free coffee and tea packets. At this price, the room probably does not have air-conditioning. The building has thin walls, several floors of rooms, steep stairs, and no elevator. Single rooms, triples, and quads will have similar features.

Breakfast is usually included in the room price, either a generous

> **$$$**   Most rooms are £125 or more.
>
>   **$$**   Most rooms between £75–125.
>
>   **$**   Most rooms £75 or less.
>
> These rates are for a standard double room during high season. Breakfast and 20 percent VAT tax is generally included in these rates.

buffet (pastries, cereal, fruit, coffee) or a full "English breakfast" of bacon-and-eggs and more.

The hotel will likely have some form of Internet access, either free or pay-as-you-go. There may be Wi-Fi in your room (to access with your own laptop or smartphone) or a public terminal in the lobby. The staff—which often includes recent immigrants—speaks at least enough English to get by. All hotels are now non-smoking.

Making Reservations

Reserve at least a few weeks in advance in peak season (June-August) or for a major holiday. Do it by email (the best way), phone, fax, or through the hotel's website. Your hotelier will want to know:

- the type of room you want (e.g., "one double room with bath")
- how many nights ("three nights")
- dates (using European format: "arriving 22/7/13, departing 25/7/13")
- any special requests ("with twin beds, air-conditioning, quiet, view")

Confirm whether breakfast and 20 percent VAT tax are included in the price. Note that an "en suite" room has a bathroom in the room, while a "standard" room has the bathroom down the hall (though there's a sink in the room).

If they require your credit-card number for a deposit, you can send it by email (I do), but it's safer via phone, fax, or the hotel's secure website. Once your room is booked, print out the confirmation, and reconfirm your reservation with a phone call a day or two in advance. If you must cancel your reservation, some hotels require advance notice or you'll be billed, but even if there's no penalty, give at least three days' notice.

Budget Tips

Some of my listed hotels offer discounts for readers of this book—it's worth asking when you book your room (look for "reader discount" in the listings that follow). To get the best deals, comparison shop by emailing several hotels or checking their websites for promo deals. You may get a cheaper rate if you pay cash, stay at least three nights, or simply ask if there are any cheaper rooms. Off-season (Nov-March), fearless negotiators can arrive without a reservation late on a slow day and start talking. Official rates can drop 30 percent, especially at pricier hotels.

Besides hotels, there are cheaper alternatives. I list a few all-ages hostels, which offer £20–30 dorm beds (and a few inexpensive doubles) and come with curfews and other rules. Bed-and-breakfasts (B&Bs) offer a private room in someone's home—try www.londonbb.com.

Renting an apartment (a "flat") can save money if you're traveling as a family, staying more than a week, and planning to cook your own meals. Try www.perfectplaces.com, www.homefromhome.co.uk, www.london 33.com, www.london-house.com, or www.gowithit.co.uk.

Looking for Hotel Deals Online

If small-hotel coziness is not your priority, you can often snag great online deals at high-rise, three- and four-star business hotels.

Big hotel chains in London: www.hilton.com, www.radisson.com, www.millenniumhotels.com, www.thistle.com, www.ichotelsgroup.com, and www.redcarnationhotels.com.

Auction-type sites: www.priceline.com and www.hotwire.com match flexible travelers with empty hotel rooms at budget prices.

Other London websites: www.londontown.com, www.lastminute.com, www.visitlondon.com, http://roomsnet.com, www.eurocheapo.com, and http://athomeinlondon.co.uk.

Don't be too cheap when picking a hotel. In summer, pay a little more for air-conditioning. And remember that cheaper places in nondescript neighborhoods can be depressing. Your London experience will be more memorable with a welcoming oasis to call home.

Sleeping

	Price	
VICTORIA STATION NEIGHBORHOOD—Central as can be; surprisingly safe, tidy, and full of decent eateries; close to Tube, bus, and train stations		
Lime Tree Hotel	$$$	Enthusiastically run, with spacious, stylish rooms and fun-loving breakfast room, free Wi-Fi
Cartref House B&B	$$	Expect rare charm and warm welcome, with 10 delightful rooms, free Wi-Fi
Morgan House	$$	Good rooms, friendly travel tips from entertaining Rachel and staff
Luna Simone Hotel	$$	Spacious modern rooms, family-run, free Wi-Fi, cash and reader discounts, handy bus #24 to Victoria Station and Trafalgar Square stops out front
New England Hotel	$$	Family-run, slightly worn but well-priced rooms in tight old corner building
Best Western Victoria Palace	$$	Modern business-class comfort in two separate buildings, air-con, free Wi-Fi
Cherry Court Hotel	$	Family-run, very small but bright rooms, air-con, free Wi-Fi, breakfast in room
Jubilee Hotel	$$	Well-run, colorful slumbermill, tiny rooms and beds, good value with reader discount
Bakers Hotel	$$	Well-worn, modest prices, tight rooms, good location, includes small breakfast, cheapest on weeknights
easyHotel Victoria	$	Franchise of modern-but-spartan hotels, super-cheap base price plus optional extras (like TV)

Address/Phone/Website/Email

135 Ebury Street, tel. 020/7730-8191, www.limetreehotel.co.uk, info@limetreehotel.co.uk

129 Ebury Street, tel. 020/7730-6176, www.cartrefhouse.co.uk, info@cartrefhouse.co.uk

120 Ebury Street, tel. 020/7730-2384, www.morganhouse.co.uk, morganhouse@btclick.com

47 Belgrave Road, tel. 020/7834-5897, www.lunasimonehotel.com, stay@lunasimonehotel.com

20 Saint George's Drive, tel. 020/7834-8351, fax 020/7834-9000, www.newenglandhotel.com, mystay@newenglandhotel.com

1 Warwick Way or 17 Belgrave Road, tel. 020/7821-7113, fax 020/7630-0806, www.bestwesternvictoriapalace.co.uk, info@bestwesternvictoriapalace.co.uk

23 Hugh Street, tel. 020/7828-2840, fax 020/7828-0393, www.cherrycourthotel.co.uk, info@cherrycourthotel.co.uk

31 Eccleston Square, tel. 020/7834-0845, www.jubileehotel.co.uk, stay@jubileehotel.co.uk

126 Warwick Way, tel. 020/7834-0729, www.bakershotel.co.uk, reservations@bakershotel.co.uk

36 Belgrave Road; Tube: Victoria, tel. 020/7834-1379, enquiries@victoria.easyhotel.com

Sleeping

	Price	
SOUTH KENSINGTON—Quiet, classy, and upscale; conveniently located on the Tube Circle Line		
Number Sixteen	$$$	Over-the-top class, modern decor, plush lounges, honeymoon-perfect, 20% VAT extra, soft prices
The Pelham Hotel	$$$	Business-class hotel mixes pretense, style, and perks (gym), 20% VAT, web specials
Aster House	$$$	Friendly owners, sunny spaces, free loaner mobile phones and Wi-Fi, reader discount
Brompton Hotel	$$	Borderline dreary, some street noise (quiet in back), breakfast in room, good price
NOTTING HILL—Residential; trendy and popular with the young international set		
Vancouver Studios	$$$	Modern rooms with equipped kitchenettes rather than breakfast, free Wi-Fi, nice garden
Phoenix Hotel	$$	Best Western modern business-class comforts (elevator, free Wi-Fi), flexible online prices
Kensington Gardens Hotel	$$	Pleasant rooms, many stairs and no elevator, breakfast next door, reader discounts
Princes Square Guest Accommodation	$$	Big well-located practical place, elevator, good value with an online discount
Westland Hotel	$$$	Great location but on a busy street, family-run, wood-paneled ambience, elevator, free Wi-Fi
London Vicarage Hotel	$$$	Family-run, elegantly British in quiet classy neighborhood, free Wi-Fi, winter discounts
The Gate Hotel	$$	Seven cramped but decent rooms near Portobello Road Market, heart of Notting Hill ambience
Norwegian YWCA (Norsk K.F.U.K.)	$	Some doubles, restrictions on age/nationality/gender, bargains worth a sex change

Address/Phone/Website/Email

16 Sumner Place, tel. 020/7589-5232, fax 020/7584-8615, US tel. 800-553-6674, www.firmdalehotels.com, sixteen@firmdale.com

15 Cromwell Place, tel. 020/7589-8288, fax 020/7584-8444, US tel. 1-888-757-5587, www.pelhamhotel.co.uk, reservations@pelhamhotel.co.uk

3 Sumner Place, tel. 020/7581-5888, fax 020/7584-4925, www.asterhouse.com, asterhouse@btinternet.com

30 Brompton Road, tel. 020/7584-4517, fax 020/7823-9936, www.bromhotel.com, book@bromhotel.com

30 Prince's Square, tel. 020/7243-1270, fax 020/7221-8678, www.vancouverstudios.co.uk, info@vancouverstudios.co.uk

1–8 Kensington Gardens Square, tel. 020/7229-2494, fax 020/7727-1419, US tel. 800-528-1234, www.phoenixhotel.co.uk, info@phoenixhotel.co.uk

9 Kensington Gardens Square, tel. 020/7243-7600, fax 020/7792-8612, www.kensingtongardenshotel.co.uk, info@kensingtongardenshotel.co.uk

23–25 Princes Square, tel. 020/7229-9876, www.princessquarehotel.co.uk, info@princessquarehotel.co.uk

154 Bayswater Road, tel. 020/7229-9191, fax 020/7727-1054, www.westlandhotel.co.uk, reservations@westlandhotel.co.uk

10 Vicarage Gate; tel. 020/7229-4030, fax 020/7792-5989, www.londonvicaragehotel.com, vicaragehotel@btconnect.com

6 Portobello Road, Tube: Noting Hill Gate, tel. 020/7221-0707, fax 020/7221-9128, www.gatehotel.co.uk, bookings@gatehotel.co.uk

52 Holland Park, Tube: Holland Park, tel. 020/7727-9346 or 020/7727-9897, www.kfukhjemmet.org.uk, kontor@kfukhjemmet.org.uk

Sleeping

	Price	
PADDINGTON STATION NEIGHBORHOOD—Not as charming, but offers all the travelers' amenities and convenient transportation connections		
St. David's Hotels	$$	Family-run hospitality, tight rooms in several adjacent buildings, free Wi-Fi
Tudor Court Hotel	$$	38 rooms, run by the Gupta family
Falcon Hotel	$$	19 small rooms wrapped around a tight staircase
easyHotel Paddington	$	Franchise of modern-but-spartan hotels, super-cheap base price plus optional extras (like TV)
The Royal Park	$$$	Classy plush rooms, polished service, free champagne, 20% VAT extra, soft prices
Stylotel	$$	39 super-modern sci-fi rooms at a good value, elevator
Olympic House Hotel	$$	39 business-class rooms with predictable comforts, elevator
NEAR EUSTON, ST. PANCRAS, AND KING'S CROSS STATIONS—Modern and conveniently located, but with little charm		
Premier Inn Kings Cross St. Pancras	$$	276 rooms, modern comforts, zero charm, online no-flex deals can be great
Premier Inn Euston	$$	Modern comforts, zero charm, packed into big blue Lego-type building, online no-flex deals can be great
Travelodge London Kings Cross	$$	Franchise with 140 modern cookie-cutter rooms, family noise, online no-flex "Saver" discounts
Hotel Ibis London Euston St. Pancras	$$	380 modern rooms on quiet street a block west of Euston Station
Jurys Inn Islington	$$$	200-plus modern, compact, comfy rooms near King's Cross Station, some online deals

14-20 Norfolk Square, tel. 020/7723-3856, fax 020/7402-9061,
www.stdavidshotels.com, info@stdavidshotels.com

10-12 Norfolk Square, tel. 020/7723-5157, fax 020/7723-0727,
www.tudorcourtpaddington.co.uk, reservations@tudorcourtpaddington.co.uk

11 Norfolk Square, tel. 020/7723-8603, www.falcon-hotel.com, info@falcon-hotel.com

10 Norfolk Place, Tube: Paddington, tel. 020/7706-9911,
enquiries@paddington.easyhotel.com

3 Westbourne Terrace, tel. 020/7479-6600, fax 020/7479-6601,
www.theroyalpark.com, info@theroyalpark.com

160-162 Sussex Gardens, tel. 020/7723-1026, www.stylotel.com, info@stylotel.com

138-140 Sussex Gardens, tel. 020/7723-5935, www.olympichousehotel.co.uk,
olympichousehotel@btinternet.com

26–30 York Way, Tube: King's Cross St. Pancras, toll tel. 0871-527-8672,
www.premierinn.com

Corner of Euston Road and Dukes Road, Tube: Euston, toll tel. 0871-527-8656,
www.premierinn.com

Grays Inn Road, Tube: King's Cross St. Pancras, toll tel. 0871-984-6256,
www.travelodge.co.uk

3 Cardington Street, tel. 020/7388-7777, fax 020/7388-0001, www.ibishotel.com,
h0921@accor.com

60 Pentonville Road, tel. 020/7282-5500, fax 020/7282-5511, www.jurysinns.com

Sleeping

	Price		
NORTH OF MARBLE ARCH—Classy and close to Oxford Street shopping			
The 22 York Street B&B	$$$	Casual alternative in urban center, traditional hardwood rooms, inviting lounge, free Wi-Fi	
The Sumner Hotel	$$$	Modern convenience and swanky extras in Georgian townhouse, near shopping, reader discount	
London Central Youth Hostel	$	Big all-ages hostel, secure and welcoming, 4- to 8-bed rooms only, kitchen	
SOUTH BANK—South of the Thames, near Shakespeare's Globe			
Premier Inn London County Hall	$$	Huge modern family-friendly franchise near London Eye, online deals	
Premier Inn London Southwark / Borough Market	$$	Near Shakespeare's Globe, alas methinks 'tis without beauty despite faire locale and bonnie pryce	

Address/Phone/Website/Email

22 York Street, tel. 020/7224-2990, www.22yorkstreet.co.uk, mc@22yorkstreet.co.uk

54 Upper Berkeley Street, tel. 020/7723-2244, fax 0870-705-8767,
www.thesumner.com, hotel@thesumner.com

104 Bolsover Street, toll tel. 0845-371-9154, www.yha.org.uk,
londoncentral@yha.org.uk

Belvedere Road, toll tel. 0871-527-8648, www.premierinn.com

34 Park Street, Tube: London Bridge, toll tel. 0871-527-8676, www.premierinn.com

Eating

England's reputation for miserable food—once well-deserved—is now history. The London cuisine scene is lively, trendy, and almost unbelievably diverse. Even traditional pub grub has gone "upmarket," offering fresh vegetables and pasta in place of greasy fries and mushy peas.

I've listed places by neighborhood—handy to your sightseeing and recommended hotels. (✪ See the restaurant maps on pages 206–209.) Because London can be expensive, I list a wide variety of eateries, from candlelit splurges to take-away fish and chips, with an emphasis on fun, moderately priced options.

Whether it's dining well with the upper-crust, sharing hearty pub fare with the blokes, or joining young secretaries at the sushi bar—eating out has become an essential part of the London experience.

Eating on London's Schedule

Traditionally, Brits have started their day with a large bacon-and-eggs breakfast. Nowadays most Londoners eat lighter, but most hotels still serve the traditional "fry," which tides many tourists over until dinner.

Lunch (12:00–2:00) is usually quick and simple—gobbling a pre-made sandwich while perched on a deli stool. Around 16:00, some Londoners still pause for the traditional tea and pastry break. After work, office drones pack London's pubs for an hour of power-drinking and noshing before the commute home. In the early evening, ethnic eateries buzz with the pre-theater crowd. After 19:00, the sit-down restaurants fill up with diners enjoying a romantic meal. Late at night, Londoners relax in the pubs for a pint, a chat, and a game of darts.

Restaurants

Traditional English fare is still served in classy, wood-paneled restaurants, but you'll find many more establishments featuring foods from around the world. All of Britain's eateries, including pubs that serve food, are now smoke-free. Get the latest on the ever-changing eating scene from weekly entertainment magazines (sold at newsstands), www.london-eating.co.uk, or www.squaremeal.co.uk.

London restaurants can be expensive when ordering a la carte. But portions are generally huge, and sharing is common. Couples could split a single main dish, a salad, and two drinks to make a filling meal.

Take advantage of fixed-price meals and specials for lunch and early-bird dinners. These can save as much as fifty percent on an a la carte meal in an elegant restaurant. (I've pointed some deals out in my listings.) Free tap water is always available.

Pub Grub

Your best bet for good, reasonably priced food is always the corner pub. Many of London's 7,000 pubs serve hearty lunches (roughly 12:00–14:00) and dinners (18:00–20:00) in friendly surroundings under ancient timbers for around £6–10. Standard items are fish and chips, "bangers and mash" (sausages and mashed potatoes), and meat pies. But many pubs now also have salad bars, quiche, hamburgers, "jacket potatoes" (baked potato with toppings), pasta, and curried dishes.

You generally order food at the bar—just ask the bartender, who can explain their pub's system. Don't tip unless the place has full table service.

Tipping

Tipping is an issue only at restaurants and fancy pubs that have waiters and waitresses. If you order food at a counter, don't tip. If the menu states that service is included, there's no need to tip beyond that. If service isn't included, tip about 10 percent by rounding up. Many restaurants in London now add a 12 percent "optional" tip onto the bill—read your bill carefully to see if service has already been included, and tip only what you think the service warrants.

Not all pubs serve meals, so look for pubs that proudly advertise their daily specials. For more pub grub listings, including upscale gastropubs (£12–18 meals), try www.thegoodpubguide.co.uk.

Pubs generally are open Monday through Saturday 11:00–23:00 and Sunday 12:00–22:30. Many stay open later, particularly on Friday and Saturday. For drinks, order your beer or other beverage at the bar and pay as you go, with no need to tip.

The pub is the heart of the people's England. Whether you're a teetotaler or a beer-guzzler, they should be a part of your travel here. "Pub" is short for "public house." It's an extended living room. Get vocal with a local. Eat, drink, get out of the rain, and watch a soccer match. A cup of darts is free for the asking. Make a few friends and memories, and feel the pulse of London. Cheers!

Other Budget Alternatives

Ethnic Restaurants: Foods from around the world—often from Britain's former colonies—add spice to the London cuisine scene. Chinese, Thai, and Middle Eastern kebabs make healthy inexpensive meals; they're even cheaper if you order take-out. Eating Indian food is practically "going local" in cosmopolitan London. If you're not familiar with Indian food, consider an easy-to-order fixed-price combination. Couples could order two main dishes, plus rice, *naan* (flatbread), and an Indian beer for about £20.

Chain Restaurants: You'll find plenty of generic franchises—Burger King, steak houses, and pizza—where you could fuel the tank for a reasonable price. Consider trying some of the interesting, non-American chains that Londoners enjoy. Wagamama Noodle Bar serves huge portions of

Taking Tea in London

Though fewer Brits these days make a big deal out of the mid-afternoon tea-and-biscuit break, many fancy restaurants and hotels offer this genteel tradition. You'll get a pot of tea with scones, jam, clotted (buttery) cream, and finger sandwiches, served in elegant, pinkie-finger surroundings. Prices range from about £10 for a small-assortment "cream" tea to a bigger £20 "afternoon" tea, to £30 or more for a "high" tea that's almost a small dinner. Some places serve tea all afternoon (12:00–18:30), some only from around 15:00 to 17:30. Most welcome tourists in jeans and sneakers. Some of my favorite places include:

- **The Wolseley,** served in a classic former car showroom (160 Piccadilly Street, Tube: Piccadilly, £10–22, reserve at tel. 020/7499-6996 or www.thewolseley.com).

- **The Orangery at Kensington Palace,** in its bright white hall near Princess Di's former residence. The portions aren't huge, but who can argue with eating at a princess' orangery or on the terrace? (in orange brick building about 100 yards from Kensington Palace, £17–25, no reservations taken, tel. 020/3166-6113, www.hrp.org.uk).

- **Fortnum & Mason** has several options: You can "Take Tea in the Parlour" for £18, enjoy the "Gallery Tea" for £26—or go all out in the new Diamond Jubilee Tea Salon, royally priced at £40-44 (181 Piccadilly, smart to reserve online or by phone at least a week ahead, tel. 0845-602-5694, www.fortnumandmason.com, dress up a bit).

- **The Capital Hotel**, a luxury hotel near Harrods' with five intimate tables (22 Basil Street, Tube: Knightsbridge, £25, definitely reserve on weekends, tel. 020/7589-5171, www.capitalhotel.co.uk).

- **The National Dining Rooms and National Café**, two less-fancy cafés in the National Gallery (Located on Trafalgar Square, Tube: Charing Cross, walk-ins welcome, £15–17, tel. 020/7747-2525, www.peytonandbyrne.co.uk).

$$$	Most meals £15–30
$$	Most meals £10–15
$	Most meals under £10

Based on the average price of a main dish and side dish at dinner, not including drinks. Eating your big meal at lunch, choosing wisely, and getting specials can often turn $$$ into $$.

reliably delicious pan-Asian food to energetic Londoners in loud, modern settings. At Yo! Sushi, freshly prepared sushi dishes trundle past on a conveyor belt. Office workers crowd Pret à Manger and "Eat" for sandwiches, salads, and pastries. Gourmet Burger Company (GBK) is popular, as is Jamie's Italian for hip, upmarket pizza and pasta. Find excellent seafood in an upscale-but-unpretentious setting at Loch Fyne Fish.

Museums: Handy on-site eateries are perfect for relaxing, and digesting all the art and culture you've taken in.

Picnics: Save time and money while enjoying London's fine park benches and polite pigeons. You can easily get prepared food to go. There's ethnic take-out, pre-made sandwiches, fish and chips, and hot-pocket-type meat pies called Cornish pasties (PASS-teez). Corner grocery chains (Sainsbury, Marks & Spencer, or Tesco) sell fruit, yogurt, trail mix, drinks, and picnic supplies. Pick up a world-class dessert at a bakery and enjoy your feast on an open-top bus tour or scenic Thames River cruise.

Some English Specialties

England's oft-maligned "cuisine" focuses on meat, potatoes, and dairy. At breakfast, sample some interesting side dishes served with the bacon-and-eggs "fry"—grilled tomato, sautéed mushrooms, or baked beans. For lunch, try various meat pies such as steak-and-kidney or shepherd's (lamb) pie. For a full-blown dinner, enjoy roast beef with Yorkshire pudding (which is a pastry, not a pudding).

Desserts, or "sweets," include a variety of sponge cakes and "puddings" (breads) slathered in cream, custard, jam, or liqueur. Many come with colorful names like fool, trifle, castle pudding, or spotted dick. Scones are popular.

Beer is a national institution. Always order on tap, not bottled, preferably from the long-handled taps, indicating it comes from casks, not kegs. The British specialty is their amber-colored ales, served warmer and less carbonated than American- and German-style lagers. Most pubs offer a variety of ales, lagers, stouts (dark, like the Irish-made Guinness), ciders (strong taste and kick), and bitters (hop-flavored ales, perhaps the most typical British beer).

Wine bars—upscale pubs serving wines by the glass—have become essentially British, but virtually no wines are homegrown. For other spirits, gentlemen enjoy the "G and T" (gin and tonic), and ladies like the fruity cocktail-in-a-bottle called Pimm's. No self-respecting bloke would order a Pimm's or a refreshing half-beer/half–7-Up "shandy." I order mine with quiche.

	Price	
CENTRAL LONDON—NEAR TRAFALGAR SQUARE (see map, pages 206–207)		
❶ St. Martin-in-the-Fields Café in the Crypt	$$	Tasty meals beneath church, cafeteria line freshly stocked for breakfast, lunch, and dinner
❷ The Chandos Pub's Opera Room	$	Fish-and-chips with locals in upstairs room overlooking Trafalgar tourist crush
❸ Gordon's Wine Bar	$$	Candlelit 15th-century cellar packed with nine-to-fivers, small-dish buffet, great with port
❹ The Lord Moon of the Mall	$	Retro English pub experience, with real ales, cheap fish-and-chips, a block from Trafalgar
CENTRAL LONDON—NEAR PICCADILLY (see map, pages 206–207)		
❺ Stockpot	$	Meat, potatoes, gravy, and mushy-peas place, with rightly popular bare-bones dinner
❻ West End Kitchen	$	Stockpot's direct competitor (same menu and prices) is just as popular
❼ Woodlands South Indian Vegetarian Restaurant	$$	Good vegetarian choice, impressive £18 *thali* (single-plate assortment)
❽ Criterion	$$$	Palatial chandelier ambience in eye-pleasing old church, reasonable for lunch, drinks, before 19:00
❾ The Wolseley	$$$	Old-time formal elegance, unexceptional but reasonable Austrian/French cuisine and tea, reservations wise

Address/Phone	Operating Hours and Days
Under the St. Martin-in-the-Fields Church, facing Trafalgar Square, Tube: Charing Cross, tel. 020/7766-1158 or 020/7766-1100	Mon–Tue 8:00–20:00, Wed 8:00–22:30, Thu–Sat 8:00–21:00, Sun 11:00–18:00
29 St. Martin's Lane, Tube: Leicester Square, tel. 020/7836-1401	Open daily 11:00–19:00
Two blocks from Trafalgar Square, bottom of Villiers Street at #47, Tube: Embankment, tel. 020/7930-1408	Mon–Sat 11:00–23:00, Sun 12:00–22:00
16–18 Whitehall, Tube: Charing Cross or Embankment, tel. 020/7839-7701	Open daily 9:00–22:00
38–40 Panton Street, tel. 020/7839-5142	Mon–Sat 7:00–23:30, Sun 7:00–22:00
5 Panton Street, tel. 020/7839-4241	Mon–Sat 7:00–23:30, Sun 7:00–22:00
37 Panton Street, tel. 020/7839-7258	Open daily 12:00–22:45, though closed 15:00–18:00 on weekdays
224 Piccadilly, tel. 020/7930-0488	Open daily 12:00–14:30 & 17:30–23:30
160 Piccadilly, tel. 020/7499-6996	Mon–Fri 7:00–24:00, Sat 8:00–24:00, Sun 8:00–23:00

Eating

		Price	
CENTRAL LONDON—NEAR COVENT GARDEN **(see map, pages 206–207)**			
10	Joe Allen	$$$	Bustling and spacious candlelit basement, modern international and American cuisine, stylish theater crowd
11	Loch Fyne Fish Restaurant	$$$	Scottish franchise, homegrown shellfish, inviting no-pretense atmosphere, £12.50 special before 18:30
12	Sofra Turkish Restaurant	$$	Quality and class, with *meze* (Turkish tapas), vegetarian, and set menu
13	Sitar Indian Restaurant	$$$	Small and dressy, with efficient service, fine fish, £17 vegetarian *thali*
14	Belgo Centraal	$$	Hearty Belgian mussels and chips in vast, underground beer-hall. Specials 17:00–18:30
15	Food for Thought	$	Packed with local vegetarians, with other cheap hippie places in nearby Neal's Yard
CENTRAL LONDON—NEAR SOHO AND CHINATOWN **(see map, pages 206–207)**			
16	Yo! Sushi	$$	Fun, popular franchise; select sushi from passing conveyor belt
17	Wagamama Noodle Bar	$	Franchise with noisy pan-Asian organic noodle dishes (everyone sucks), huge splittable portions
18	Busaba Eathai	$	Join happy locals crowding around 16-seat communal tables for tasty Thai, some two-person tables
19	Côte Restaurant	$$	Contemporary French bistro chain, good-value, no pretense
20	Y Ming Chinese Restaurant	$$	Dressy European decor, authentic northern Chinese cooking, serious but helpful service
21	New World Chinese Restaurant	$	Chinatown fixture, sprawling old-fashioned diner, cheap Cantonese dim sum and more

Address/Phone	Operating Hours and Days
13 Exeter Street, tel. 020/7836-0651	Open daily 11:30–24:30, piano music after 21:00
A couple of blocks behind Covent Garden at 2 Catherine Street, tel. 020/7240-4999	Open daily
36 Tavistock Street, tel. 020/7240-3773	Open daily 9:00–24:00
Next to Somerset House at 149 Strand, tel. 020/7836-3730	Mon–Fri 12:00–24:00, Sat–Sun 14:30–24:00
One block north of Covent Garden Tube station at 50 Earlham Street, tel. 020/7813-2233	Open daily 12:00–23:00
31 Neal Street: 2 blocks north of Covent Garden Tube station, near Neal's Yard, tel. 020/7836-0239	Mon–Sat 12:00–20:30, Sun 12:00–17:30
52 Poland Street: 2 blocks south of Oxford Street, where Lexington Street becomes Poland Street, tel. 020/7287-0443	Open daily 12:00–23:00
10A Lexington Street, tel. 020/7292-0990	Mon–Sat 11:30–23:00, Sun 12:00–22:00
106 Wardour Street, tel. 020/7255-8686; Other locations: on nearby Panton Street, at 22 Store Street, and 8-13 Bird Street	Mon–Thu 12:00–23:00, Fri–Sat 12:00–23:30, Sun 12:00–22:30
124–126 Wardour Street, tel. 020/7287-9280	Mon–Wed 8:00–23:00, Thu–Fri 8:00–24:00, Sat 9:00–24:00, Sun 10:00–22:30
35–36 Greek Street, tel. 020/7734-2721	Mon–Sat 12:00–23:45, closed Sun
1 Gerrard Place, tel. 020/7734-0677	Open daily 12:00–24:00

Eating

Eating

		Price	
CENTRAL LONDON—NEAR SOHO AND CHINATOWN (see map, pages 206–207)			
22	Andrew Edmunds Restaurant	$$$	Tiny candlelit local find, modern European cuisine, splurge-worthy, reserve ground floor table
23	Mildred's Vegetarian Restaurant	$	Enjoyable menu, pleasant interior, vegan options, happy eaters
24	Fernandez & Wells	$	Simple little wine bar, sandwiches for lunch, ham and cheese plates after 16:00
THE CITY, AROUND ST. PAUL'S (see map, page 208)			
25	The Counting House	$	Pub with modern touch, "nibbles menu" for after-work crowd
26	De Gustibus Sandwiches	$	Artisan bakery for sandwiches, salads, soups, take-away or stay
27	Ye Olde Cheshire Cheese	$	1667 tavern once served pub grub to Dickens, Samuel Johnson, Yeats
28	The Black Friar	$	Great Art Nouveau decor (c. 1900–1915) and traditional pub fare
29	The Old Bank of England	$	Pub in lavish old bank building
NOTTING HILL (see map, page 208)			
30	Maggie Jones's	$$$	Solid English cuisine, rustic but jazzy ambience, huge splittable meat-and-fish pies
31	The Churchill Arms and Thai Kitchen	$	Old-English pub grub in front, hearty Thai in back, packed 18:00–21:00
32	The Prince Edward	$	Cut-above grub in classic pub setting, indoor or sidewalk tables
33	Café Diana	$	Healthy Middle Eastern pita sandwiches, salads, and meals

Address/Phone	Operating Hours and Days
46 Lexington Street, tel. 020/7437-5708	Mon–Sat 12:30–15:00 & 18:00–22:45, Sun 13:00–15:30 & 18:00–22:30
45 Lexington Street, tel. 020/7494-1634	Mon–Sat 12:00–23:00, closed Sun
43 Lexington Street, tel. 020/7734-1546	Open daily 11:00–22:00
50 Cornhill, east of St. Paul's, near Mansion House, tel. 020/7283-7123	Mon–Fri 9:00–23:00, closed Sat–Sun
53–55 Carter Lane, from church steps follow signs to youth hostel a block downhill, tel. 020/7236-0056	Mon–Fri 7:00–17:00, closed Sat–Sun
145 Fleet Street, Tube: Temple or St. Paul's, tel. 020/7353-6170	Open daily
174 Queen Victoria Street, tel. 020/7236-5474	Open daily 10:00–23:00
194 Fleet Street, Tube: Temple, tel. 020/7430-2255	Mon–Fri 11:00–23:00, closed Sat–Sun
6 Old Court Place, just east of Kensington Church Street, near High Street Kensington Tube stop, tel. 020/7937-6462	Mon–Sat 12:30–15:00 & 18:00–23:00, Sun 12:00–15:00 & 18:00–22:30
119 Kensington Church Street, tel. 020/7792-1246	Open daily 12:00–22:00
73 Prince's Square: 2 blocks north of Bayswater Road at the corner of Dawson Place and Hereford Road, tel. 020/7727-2221	Mon–Wed 10:00–23:00, Thu–Sat 10:00–23:30, Sun 10:00–22:30
5 Wellington Terrace, on Bayswater Road: opposite Kensington Palace Garden Gates, tel. 020/7792-9606	Open daily 8:00–23:00

Eating

		Price	
NOTTING HILL **(see map, page 208)**			
34	Royal China Restaurant	$$	Pricey favorite for dress-up Chinese locals, dim sum until 17:00
35	Whiteleys Shopping Centre Food Court	$	Options include Yo! Sushi, Café Rouge, pizza, Starbucks
36	Tesco Supermarket	$	Grocery store a half-block from Notting Hill Gate Tube stop
SOUTH KENSINGTON **(see map, page 209)**			
37	La Bouchée Bistro Café	$$$	Classy French hole-in-the-wall, £11.50 special weekdays 12:00–13:00 and 17:30–18:30
38	Gessler at Daquise	$$	Polish kielbasa and kraut, weekday lunch special
39	Moti Mahal Indian Restaurant	$$	Bangladeshi, mod ambience, good service, try spicy chicken *jalfrezi*
40	Beirut Express	$$	Fresh Lebanese cuisine, cheap take-away in front, restaurant in back
41	Bosphorus Kebabs	$	Student favorite for quick hearty Turkish meals and kebobs
42	Rocca di Papa	$$	Bright and dressy Italian place with heated terrace, £8 pizza, pasta, or salad
43	The Anglesea Arms	$$$	Destination pub, great terrace, mellow woody ambience, gourmet pub cuisine
44	Tesco Express Supermarket	$	Grocery with late hours, handy for picnics

Address/Phone	Operating Hours and Days
13 Queensway, tel. 020/7221-2535	Mon–Thu 12:00–23:00, Fri–Sat 12:00–23:30, Sun 11:00–22:00
Second floor, corner of Porchester Gardens and Queensway	Open daily 8:30–24:00
114–120 Notting Hill Gate: near intersection with Pembridge Road	Mon–Sat 7:00–23:00, Sun 12:00–18:00
56 Old Brompton Road, tel. 020/7589-1929	Open daily 12:00–15:00 & 17:00–23:00
20 Thurloe Street, tel. 020/7589-6117	Open daily 12:00–23:00
3 Glendower Place, tel. 020/7584-8428	Open daily 12:00–14:30 & 17:30–23:00
65 Old Brompton Road, tel. 020/7591-0123	Open daily 12:00–23:00
59 Old Brompton Road, tel. 020/7584-4048	Open daily 10:30–24:00
73 Old Brompton Road, tel. 020/7225-3413	Open daily 11:30–23:30
15 Selwood Terrace: a couple of blocks off Old Brompton Road, tel. 020/7373-7960	Meals served daily 12:00–15:00 & 18:30–22:00
50–52 Old Brompton Road	Open daily 7:00–24:00

Eating

Eating

	Price	
VICTORIA STATION NEIGHBORHOOD (see map, page 209)		
⑤ Ebury Wine Bar	$$$	Upscale young professionals enjoy cut-above pub grub or pricey French cuisine
⑥ Jenny Lo's Tea House	$	Reliable, eclectic Chinese for locals in the know, small menu, high quality
⑦ La Bottega	$	Upscale Italian deli for fresh pastas, salads, sandwiches, to go or stay
⑧ The Duke of Wellington	$	Classic neighborhood pub, forgettable grub, woodsy sidewalk seating, inviting interior
⑨ The Thomas Cubitt	$$$	Trendy upscale gastropub for young professionals, small-plate bar menu, pricey meals
⑩ Grumbles	$$$	Unpretentious cozy booths, excellent traditional English dishes, £10 specials 18:00–19:00
⑪ Seafresh Fish Restaurant	$$	Family-run with classic and creative fish-and-chips, £5 take-out
⑫ The Jugged Hare	$	Vivid pub scene in old bank building, traditional grub plus modern veggies
⑬ St. George's Tavern	$	First-rate pub, eat inside or out, try "toad in the hole" sausages
⑭ Marks & Spencer and ⑮ Sainsbury Market	$	Two grocery stores with long hours, located inside Victoria Station

Address/Phone	Operating Hours and Days
139 Ebury Street: at intersection of Ebury and Elizabeth Streets, tel. 020/7730-5447	Open daily 12:00–14:45 & 18:00–22:15
14 Eccleston Street, tel. 020/7259-0399	Mon–Fri 12:00–14:45 & 18:00–22:00, closed Sat–Sun
On corner of Ebury and Eccleston Streets, tel. 020/7730-2730	Mon–Fri 8:00–19:00, Sat 9:00–18:00, Sun 9:00–17:00
63 Eaton Terrace, tel. 020/7730-1782	Food served Mon–Sat 12:00–15:00 & 18:00–21:00, Sun lunch only
44 Elizabeth Street, tel. 020/7730-6060	Bar menu daily 12:00–21:45
35 Churton Street, half a block north of Belgrave Road, tel. 020/7834-0149	Open daily 12:00–14:30 & 18:00–23:00
80–81 Wilton Road, tel. 020/7828-0747	Mon–Sat 12:00–15:00 & 17:00–22:30, closed Sun
172 Vauxhall Bridge Road, tel. 020/7828-1543	Food served Mon–Sat 12:00–22:00, Sun until 21:30
Corner of Hugh Street and Belgrave Road, tel. 020/7630-1116	Mon–Sat 10:00–22:00, Sun until 21:30
Both stores located inside Victoria Station, Sainsbury Market at rear entrance, on Eccleston Street	Marks & Spencer: Mon–Sat 7:00–24:00, Sun 8:00–22:00; Sainsbury's Market: daily 6:00–23:00

Central London Restaurants

Eating

Rick Steves' | Pocket London

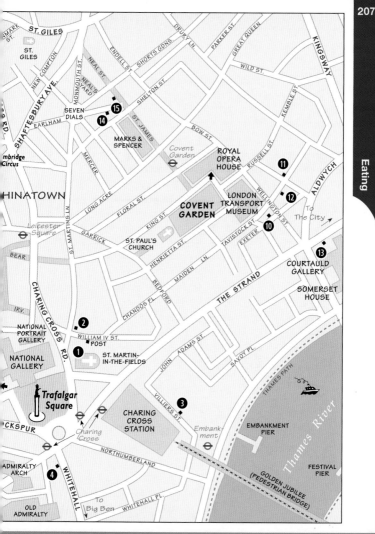

ST. GILES

ST. GILES

NMARK

NEW COMPTON

SHAFTESBURY AVE.

RD.

EARLHAM

MERCER

ST. MARTIN'S LN.

GARRICK

BEAR

CHARING CROSS RD.

IRV.

NATIONAL PORTRAIT GALLERY

NATIONAL GALLERY

CKSPUR

Trafalgar Square

ADMIRALTY ARCH

OLD ADMIRALTY

mbridge Circus

HINATOWN

Leicester Square

MONMOUTH ST.

NEAL ST.

NEAL'S YARD

SEVEN DIALS

14

15

ENDELL'S

SHORTS GDNS

SHELTON ST.

ST. JAMES

MARKS & SPENCER

LONG ACRE

FLORAL ST.

KING ST.

ST. PAUL'S CHURCH

BEDFORD

CHANDOS PL.

HENRIETTA ST.

MAIDEN LN.

2

WILLIAM IV ST.
POST

1

ST. MARTIN-IN-THE-FIELDS

Charing Cross

CHARING CROSS STATION

VILLIERS ST.

3

JOHN ADAMS ST.

Embankment

NORTHUMBERLAND

WHITEHALL

4

To Big Ben

WHITEHALL PL.

DRURY LN.

PARKER ST.

GREAT QUEEN

WILD ST.

KINGSWAY

BOW ST.

Covent Garden

ROYAL OPERA HOUSE

COVENT GARDEN

LONDON TRANSPORT MUSEUM

TAVISTOCK ST.

EXETER ST.

10

KEMBLE ST.

RUSSELL ST.

11

WELLINGTON ST.

12

ALDWYCH

To The City

13

COURTAULD GALLERY

SOMERSET HOUSE

THE STRAND

SAVOY PL.

THAMES PATH

Thames River

EMBANKMENT PIER

FESTIVAL PIER

GOLDEN JUBILEE (PEDESTRIAN BRIDGE)

Eating

Restaurants Around St. Paul's

200 Meters
200 Yards

ROYAL COURTS OF JUSTICE
29
FETTER
27
OLD BAILEY
ST. PAUL'S
St. Paul's
GRESHAM ST.
THE CITY
KING
BANK
THREAD
FLEET ST.
MITRE CT.
City Thameslink
CHEAPSIDE
Bank
CORNHILL
25
CARTER LANE
26
Mansion House
WILLIAM
THE TEMPLE
28
Blackfriars
CANNON ST.
VICTORIA EMBANKMENT
UPPER THAMES ST.
CANNON STREET STATION
Monument
BLACK-FRIARS PIER
BLACK-FRIARS BRIDGE
Thames River
MILLENNIUM BRIDGE

Notting Hill Restaurants

200 Meters
200 Yards

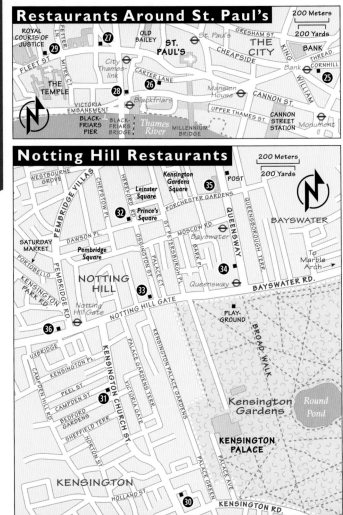

WESTBOURNE GROVE
PEMBRIDGE VILLAS
CHEPSTOW RD.
HEREFORD
Leinster Square
Kensington Gardens Square
35
POST
PORCHESTER GARDENS
BAYSWATER
32
Prince's Square
ST. PETERSBURGH PL.
MOSCOW RD.
Bayswater
QUEENSWAY
QUEENSBOROUGH TERR.
To Marble Arch
SATURDAY MARKET
DAWSON PL.
Pembridge Square
OSSINGTON ST.
PALACE CT.
BARK PL.
34
PORTOBELLO
PEMBRIDGE RD.
NOTTING HILL
33
Queensway
BAYSWATER RD.
KENSINGTON PARK RD.
Notting Hill Gate
NOTTING HILL GATE
PLAY-GROUND
BROAD WALK
36
UXBRIDGE
CAMPDEN HILL RD.
KENSINGTON PL.
PEEL ST.
CAMPDEN ST.
31
Bedford Gardens
SHEFFIELD TERR.
HORTON ST.
KENSINGTON CHURCH ST.
VICTORIA GATE
KENSINGTON PALACE GARDENS
PALACE GARDENS TERR.
Kensington Gardens
Round Pond
KENSINGTON PALACE
KENSINGTON
HOLLAND ST.
30
PALACE GREEN
PALACE AVE.
KENSINGTON RD.

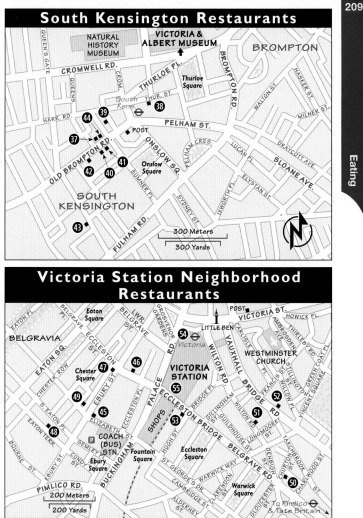

South Kensington Restaurants

NATURAL HISTORY MUSEUM

VICTORIA & ALBERT MUSEUM

BROMPTON

QUEEN'S GATE

CROMWELL RD.

QUEEN'S GATE

THURLOE PL.

Thurloe Square

BROMPTON RD.

WALTON ST.

HASKER ST.

MILNER ST.

South Kens

THUR. ST.

HARR. RD.

44 39

38

PELHAM ST.

PELHAM CRES.

LUCAN PL.

DRAYCOTT AVE.

SLOANE AVE.

37

POST

ONSLOW SQ.

Onslow Square

ELYSTAN ST.

OLD BROMPTON RD.

42 40 41

SUMNER PL.

HAWORTH ST.

SYDNEY ST.

SOUTH KENSINGTON

43

FULHAM RD.

300 Meters

300 Yards

N

Victoria Station Neighborhood Restaurants

EATON PL.

BELGRAVE PL.

Eaton Square

LWR. BELGRAVE ST.

GROSVENOR GARDENS

POST

Victoria

VICTORIA ST.

HOWICK PL.

LITTLE BEN

CARLISLE PL.

AMBROSDEN AVE.

THIRLEBY RD.

BELGRAVIA

EATON SQ.

ECCLESTON ST.

54

WILTON RD.

VAUXHALL BRIDGE RD.

FRANCIS ST.

WESTMINSTER CHURCH

VINCENT SQUARE

CHESTER ROW

Chester Square

47

46

VICTORIA STATION

49

EBURY ST.

ECCLESTON PL.

55

PALACE ST.

ECCLESTON BRIDGE

BRIDGE PL.

GILLINGHAM ST.

GUILDHOUSE ST.

WILTON RD.

LONGMOORE ST.

52

51

45

ELIZABETH ST.

SHOPS

53

HUGH ST.

S. EATON PL.

48

COACH (BUS) STN.

SEMLEY PL.

Ebury Square

Fountain Square

Eccleston Square

BELGRAVE RD.

DENBIGH ST.

TACHBROOK ST.

CHARLWOOD ST.

BOURNE ST.

EBURY ST.

CUNDY ST.

BUCKINGHAM

ST. GEORGE'S DR.

WARWICK WAY

Warwick Square

50

GLOUCESTER ST.

PIMLICO RD.

200 Meters

200 Yards

CAMBRIDGE ST.

CLARENDON ST.

ALDERNEY ST.

To Pimlico & Tate Britain

Rick Steves' | Pocket London

Practicalities

Helpful Websites

London Tourist Information: www.visitlondon.com
Britain Tourist Information: www.visitbritain.com
Passports and Red Tape: www.travel.state.gov
Cheap Flights: www.skyscanner.net
Airplane Carry-on Restrictions: www.tsa.gov/travelers
London Entertainment and Current Events: www.timeout.com
/london or www.londontown.com
European Train Schedules: http://bahn.hafas.de/bin/query.exe/en
General Travel Tips: For information on riding the trains, railpasses, car rental, travel insurance, packing lists, and much more—as well as updates for this book—see www.ricksteves.com

PLANNING

When to Go

London's best travel months are July and August, with the best weather, daylight from 6:30–22:00, and the full range of tourist activities. "Shoulder season" (May–June, Sept–early Oct) has slightly smaller crowds and slightly better hotel prices, and the weather is decent. London makes a great winter getaway, especially during Christmas season. Although it's dark and drizzly, you'll find fewer crowds. The pubs are cozy and the city feels lively but not touristy. No matter when you go, plan for rain.

Before You Go

You need a passport (see www.travel.state.gov). Call your debit and credit card companies about your plans (see below). Book hotel rooms well in advance during peak season (July–Aug and three-day weekends) and consider buying travel insurance. Research railpasses, Eurostar train reservations, and car rentals.

MONEY

Britain's currency is the pound sterling. One British pound (£1) = about $1.60. To convert pounds to dollars add 60 percent: £20 = about $32, £50 = about $80. (Check www.oanda.com for the latest exchange rates.) The pound, also called a "quid," is broken into 100 pence (p).

Withdraw money from an ATM (often called a "cashpoint" in Britain) using a debit card, just like at home. Visa and MasterCard are most commonly used throughout Europe. Before departing, call your bank or credit-card company: Confirm that your card will work overseas, ask about international transaction fees, and alert them that you'll be making withdrawals in Europe.

Be aware that—while American credit cards are accepted almost everywhere in Europe—they may not work in some European vending machines (e.g. buying train tickets from a machine). But don't freak out. You can pay with cash, try your PIN code (ask your credit-card company in advance or use a debit card), or find a nearby cashier who should be able to process the transaction.

Refuse any offers from merchants to charge your purchase in dollars (called "dynamic currency conversion")—it's a needless rip-off.

To keep your valuables safe, wear a money belt. But if you do lose your credit or debit card, report the loss immediately with a phone call: Visa (tel. 303/967-1096), MasterCard (tel. 636/722-7111), and American Express (tel. 623/492-8427).

ARRIVAL IN LONDON

Heathrow Airport

One of the world's busiest airports, Heathrow has five terminals, T-1 through T-5. Each terminal has all the necessary travelers' services (info desks, ATMs, shops, eateries, etc). You can travel between terminals on free trains and buses, but it can be time-consuming—plan ahead if you'll need to change terminals. For airport and flight information, call toll tel. 0844-335-1801 or visit www.heathrowairport.com.

To get between Heathrow and downtown London (14 miles away), you have several options:

Taxi: The one-hour trip costs £45–75 to west and central London, for up to four people. Just get in the queue outside the terminal.

Tube: For £5.50, the Tube takes you from any Heathrow terminal to downtown London in 50–60 minutes on the Piccadilly Line (6/hour). Follow signs in the terminal to the Tube station. Before buying a Heathrow-to-London ticket, consider buying an Oyster Card or Travelcard covering Zone 1-2 (central London) and paying a small supplement for the Heathrow-to-London portion.

Train: From terminals T-1 and T-3, the Heathrow Connect train goes to Paddington Station (£9.50, £5 more to buy onboard, 2/hour, 30 minutes, toll tel. 0845-678-6975, www.heathrowconnect.com). From T-1, T-3, and T-5, the Heathrow Express goes to Paddington (£19, 4/hour, 15–20 minutes, toll tel. 0845-600-1515, www.heathrowexpress.co.uk).

Bus: Terminals T-1 and T-3 have a bus station outside, where National Express buses go to Victoria Coach Station near the Victoria train and Tube station (£6–9, 1–2/hour, 45–75 minutes, toll tel. 0871-781-8178, www.nationalexpress.com).

Airporter Vans: These share-the-ride shuttle vans work like those at home, carrying passengers directly to or from their hotel. Heathrow Shuttle serves all terminals (£18/person, reservations toll tell. 0845-257-8068, www.heathrowshuttle.com).

From London to Heathrow: To get to Heathrow from your hotel, your transportation options are the same as above, but here are a few tips. Confirm with your airline in advance which terminal your flight will use, to avoid having to transfer between terminals. If arriving by Tube, note that not every Piccadilly Line train stops at every terminal. Before boarding, make sure your train is going to the terminal you want. A taxi arranged through your hotel can often be cheaper (£30–40) than from Heathrow to London. Bold negotiators may do even better by flagging a cab down on the street and asking for their best "off-meter" rate.

Gatwick and London's Other Airports

Of London's five airports, Gatwick is second-biggest (toll tel. 0844-892-0322, www.gatwickairport.com). To get from Gatwick into London, Gatwick Express trains shuttle conveniently to Victoria Station (£19, £33 round-trip, 4/hour, 30 minutes, toll tel. 0845-850-1530, www.gatwick express.com). To connect Gatwick and Heathrow, use the National Express bus (£20–25, 75-minute trip, allow at least three hours between flights, toll tel. 0871-781-8178, www.nationalexpress.com).

London's other, lesser airports are Stansted Airport (toll tel. 0844-335-1803, www.stanstedairport.com), Luton Airport (tel. 01582/405-100, www.london-luton.co.uk), and London City Airport (tel. 020/7646-0088, www.londoncityairport.com).

London's Train Stations

There are nine main stations, each serving a different region. For example, to go to Paris on the Eurostar, you leave from St. Pancras International. Trains to Heathrow, Windsor, or Bath leave from Paddington. Any train station can make reservations and sell tickets for any destination.

For schedules, tickets, and general information on British trains, call 0845-748-4950 or visit www.nationalrail.co.uk. The best all-Europe train schedule information is at http://bahn.hafas.de/bin/query.exe/en. To see if a railpass could save you money, check www.ricksteves.com/rail.

Eurostar: High-speed trains from St. Pancras International zip you under the English Channel to Paris or Brussels in 2.5 hours. Prices can range from $460 (first-class full-fare tickets) to less than $100 (second-class, non-refundable specials), so do your research and book ahead for the best deals. Visit www.raileurope.com, www.eurostar.com, or read my *Guide to Eurail Passes* at www.ricksteves.com/eurostar.

By Bus—Victoria Coach Station: For travel beyond London, buses are a cheaper—but considerably slower—option than the train. Most depart from Victoria Coach Station, which is one long block south of Victoria Station (Tube: Victoria, toll tel. 0871-781-8178 or www.nationalexpress .com).

HELPFUL HINTS

Tourist Information (TI): London's only publicly funded (and therefore impartial) TI is the City of London Information Centre, just south of St. Paul's Cathedral. Get your travel questions answered and choose from dozens of free brochures, including the *London Planner* monthly events guide. They sell advance tickets and skip-the-queue Fast Track tickets to big, crowded sights (including Madame Tussauds, which is discounted here). You can also buy sightseeing passes and buy theater tickets (20 percent booking fee). It's located at St. Paul's Churchyard (Mon–Sat 9:30–17:30, Sun 10:00–16:00, Tube: St. Paul's, www.visitthecity.co.uk). Other "tourist information" agencies around town are either for-profit ticket- and tour-sales offices or ones offering only public-transit advice.

The best travel bookstores are Stanfords (12–14 Long Acre, Tube: Leicester Square, www.stanfords.co.uk) and Waterstone's (locations on both Piccadilly and Trafalgar Squares). The *Benson's London Street Map* (£2.75) is my favorite.

Time: Britain uses the 24-hour clock. It's the same through 12:00 noon, then keeps going: 13:00, 14:00, and so on. Britain's time zone is one hour earlier than most of continental Europe, which makes it five/eight hours ahead of the east/west coasts of the US.

Business Hours: Most stores are open Monday through Saturday (roughly 10:00–17:00), with a late night on Wednesday or Thursday (until 19:00 or 20:00), depending on the neighborhood. On Sunday, when some stores are closed, street markets are lively with shoppers. Handy hole-in-the-wall grocery stores stay open late every day.

Numbers and Stumblers: What Americans call the second floor of a building is the first floor in Europe. Europeans write dates as day/month/year, so Christmas is 25/12/13. Commas are decimal points and vice versa—a dollar and a half is 1,50, and there are 5.280 feet in a mile.

Britain uses a mix of "our" Imperial system (pounds, miles) and the metric system: A kilogram is 2.2 pounds; a liter is about a quart; and a kilometer is six-tenths of a mile. The British measure temperature in Celsius. 0°C = 32°F. For a rough conversion from Celsius to Fahrenheit, double the number and add 30.

Holidays and Weekends: London's always-busy sights are inundated on three-day weekends, especially Bank Holidays on the first and

Tipping

Tipping in Britain isn't as generous as it is in the US. In restaurants (or pubs with table service), check the menu or your bill to see if the service is already included; if not, tip about 10 percent. At pubs where you order at the counter, you don't have to tip.

To tip the cabbie, round up, to about 10 percent (for a £4.50 fare, give £5).

At hotels, if you let the porter carry your luggage, give them 50p for each bag. I don't tip the maid, but if you do, you can leave 50p per night at the end of your stay.

last Mondays in May, and the last Monday in August. For a good list, visit www.visitlondon.com/travel/public-holidays.

Watt's Up? Britain's electrical system operates on 220 volts (rather than 110 in the US) and uses plugs with three square prongs (rather than America's two slots or continental Europe's two round prongs). You'll need a three-prong adapter plug, sold inexpensively at travel stores in the US, and in British airports and drugstores. Most newer electronics automatically convert the voltage, so you won't need a separate converter.

Discounts: Many British sights, buses, and trains offer discounts (called "concessions" or "concs") for seniors (loosely defined as those who are retired or willing to call themselves a senior), children, families, and students and teachers with an international ID card (see www.isic.org).

Pedestrian Safety: Cars drive on the left side of the road—which can be as confusing for foreign pedestrians as for foreign drivers. Before crossing a street, I always look right, look left, then look right again just to be sure. Most crosswalks are even painted with instructions, reminding foreign guests to "Look right" or "Look left."

Hurdling the Language Barrier: Don't get fagged or wound up over the twee, homely way Joe Bloggs can witter on. I mean, Bob's your uncle, we speak the same language. But if you do have trouble decoding how the English speak English, ✪ see the British-Yankee Vocabulary list on page 234. And please...don't call your waist pack a "fanny pack."

GETTING AROUND LONDON

In London, you're never more than a 10-minute walk from a stop on the metro/subway system (called the Tube). Buses are also convenient, and taxis are everywhere. For public transit info, see www.tfl.gov.uk.

Buying Tickets and Public-Transit Passes

A single ticket to ride the Tube costs a whopping £4.50, and buses are £2.40. Save money with a pass, which covers both the Tube and the bus system.

Oyster Card: This pay-as-you-go plastic debit card lets you travel at about half the price per ride as single Tube or bus tickets. You must pay a £5 (refundable) deposit when you buy the card, then load it up with as

Practicalities

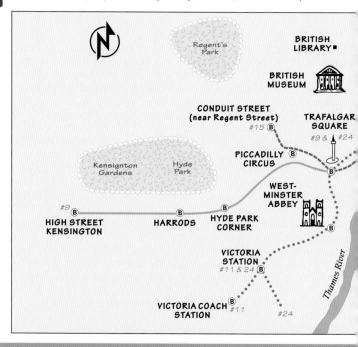

much credit as you want. I start with about £10 for a three-day stay. When your balance gets low, you simply add credit—or "top up"—at a ticket window or machine. To use it, you simply touch the card to the turnstile/reader when you enter the Tube system or board the bus. The cost of the ride is automatically deducted from your account. No matter how much you travel in a 24-hour period, you never pay more than £8.80.

One-Day Travelcard: This pass gives unlimited travel on the Tube and buses for a day for £8.80. (The £7 off-peak version is good for travel after 9:30 on weekdays and anytime on weekends.) To use it, feed the Travelcard into the Tube turnstile like a paper ticket (and retrieve it), or show it to the bus driver.

Seven-Day Travelcard: For £30.40 (plus a refundable £5 deposit), you get a week's worth of travel. It's issued on a plastic Oyster card.

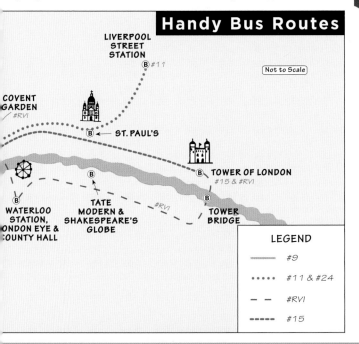

Handy Bus Routes

LIVERPOOL STREET STATION
Ⓑ #11

Not to Scale

COVENT GARDEN
#RVI

Ⓑ ← ST. PAUL'S

TOWER OF LONDON
Ⓑ #15 & #RVI

Ⓑ

#RVI

Ⓑ
WATERLOO STATION, LONDON EYE & COUNTY HALL

TATE MODERN & SHAKESPEARE'S GLOBE

Ⓑ
TOWER BRIDGE

LEGEND

═══	#9
•••••	#11 & #24
─ ─	#RVI
-----	#15

Which Pass is Best? For three days or fewer, consider One-Day Travelcards for each day you'll be taking more than one Tube ride. The pay-as-you-go Oyster card also works for a short visit. For four days or longer, get either the Seven-Day Travelcard (which can pay for itself in four busy days) or the pay-as-you-go Oyster.

Buy Oyster Cards and Travelcards at any Tube station, from a ticket window or vending machine. All of these passes cover the Tube and bus system within Zones 1 and 2—an area that stretches beyond the Circle Line and includes virtually all recommended sights. For more detailed info on tickets, passes, and prices, see www.tfl.gov.uk.

By Tube

Called the Tube or Underground (but never "subway"), one of this planet's great people-movers runs Monday through Saturday about 5:00–24:00, Sunday about 7:00–23:00. Begin by studying the Tube side of the foldout map at the back of this book.

Each line has a name (such as Circle, Northern, or Bakerloo) and two directions (indicated by the end-of-the-line stops). Find the line that will take you to your destination, and figure out roughly what direction (north, south, east, or west) you'll need to go to get there.

In the Tube station, use your Oyster Card, Travelcard, or ticket to pass through the turnstile. Find your train by following signs to your line and the direction it's headed (such as "Central Line: east"). Since some tracks are shared by several lines, read signs on the platform to confirm that the approaching train is going to your specific destination. Transfers to another train are free, until you reach your final destination. You'll need your Oyster, Travelcard, or ticket to pass through the exit turnstile. Save walking time by choosing the best street exit—check the maps on the walls or ask any station personnel.

Rush hours (8:00–10:00 and 16:00–19:00) can be packed and sweaty. Be prepared to walk significant distances within Tube stations and ride long escalators (stand on the right to let others pass). Delays are common; bring something to pass the time. Be wary of thieves, especially amid the jostle of boarding and leaving crowded trains. For more info on the Tube, see www.tfl.gov.uk.

By Bus

London's excellent bus system works like buses anywhere. Every bus stop has a name, and every bus is headed to one end-of-the-line stop or the other. Buses are covered by Travelcards and Oyster cards. Or you can buy single-trip tickets (£2.40) from a machine at bus stops.

As you board, show your ticket or Travelcard to the driver, or touch your Oyster card to the card reader. There's no need to tap your card or show your ticket when you hop off.

If you have an Oyster card or Travelcard, save your feet and use the bus, even just to get to a Tube stop. Check the bus stop closest to your hotel—it might be convenient to your sightseeing plans. During bump-and-grind rush hours (8:00–10:00 and 16:00–19:00), you'll go faster by Tube.

A few bus routes handy to sights and recommended hotels are:

Route #15: This east-west route (using some old-style double-decker buses) runs from Regent Street to Piccadilly and Trafalgar Square, then continues along Fleet Street to St. Paul's and the Tower of London.

Route #9: Runs east-west (on double-decker buses) along the southern border of Hyde Park to Piccadilly Circus and Trafalgar Square.

Routes #11 and #24: Victoria Station to Westminster Abbey to Trafalgar Square (#11 continues to St. Paul's).

Route #RV1: A scenic South Bank joyride, it goes east-west from the Tower of London to the London Eye, then back across the Thames to Covent Garden.

By Taxi

London is the best taxi town in Europe. Big, black cabs are everywhere, and there's no meter-cheating. They know every nook and cranny in town. I've never met a crabby cabbie.

If a cab's top light is on, just wave it down—even cabs going the opposite way—or find the nearest taxi stand. Telephoning a cab will get you one in minutes, but costs about £2–3 more (toll tel. 0871-871-8710).

Rides start at £2.40. The rate goes up about 20 percent after 20:00, and another 20 percent after 22:00. All extra charges are explained in writing on the cab wall. Tip a cabbie by rounding up (maximum 10 percent).

A typical daytime trip—from Trafalgar Square to St. Paul's—costs about £10. All cabs can carry five passengers, and some take six, for the same cost as a single traveler. So for a short ride, three adults in a cab travel at close to Tube prices. Avoid cabs when traffic is bad—they're slow and expensive, because the meter keeps running even at a standstill.

COMMUNICATING

Telephones

Making Calls: To call Britain from the US or Canada: Dial 011-44 and then the local number, without the initial zero. (The 011 is our international access code, and 44 is Britain's country code.)

To call Britain from a European country: Dial 00-44 followed by the local number, without the initial zero. (The 00 is Europe's international access code.)

To call within Britain: If you're dialing within an area code, just dial the local number (without the area code). Otherwise dial both the area code (including the initial 0) and the local number.

To call from Britain to another country: Dial 00 followed by the country code (for example, 1 for the US or Canada), then the area code and number. If you're calling European countries whose phone numbers begin with 0, you'll usually have to omit that 0 when you dial.

Phoning Inexpensively: London still has a reasonable number of payphones. They accept both coins (minimum toll 40p) and major credit cards (which you physically insert into the phone).

To make international calls, the cheapest option is using an international phone card, which works with a scratch-to-reveal PIN code. This gives you pennies-per-minute rates on international calls, decent rates for calls within Britain, and can even be used from your mobile phone or your hotel phone. (Unfortunately, you get poor rates when used from payphones. Also, some hotels block the cards' toll-free access numbers, so you end up paying some hotel charges.) Buy international phone cards at newsstands and groceries (£5). Tell the vendor where you'll be making the most calls ("to the States"), and he'll select a good-value brand. Calling from your hotel room can be a rip-off for long-distance calls unless you use an international phone card—ask your hotelier about rates before using the hotel phone.

Mobile Phones: A mobile phone—whether an American one that works in Britain, or a European one you buy when you arrive—is increasingly affordable. You'll find mobile-phone stores selling cheap phones (for as little as $20 plus minutes) and SIM cards, at Heathrow airport, major train stations, and throughout London.

Many smartphones, such as the iPhone or Android, work in Europe—but beware of sky-high fees, especially for data downloading (checking email, browsing the Internet, watching videos). The simplest way to use

Useful Phone Numbers

Police and Ambulance: tel. 999
Operator Assistance: 100 (free)
Directory Assistance: 118-500 (70p per minute)
International Directory Assistance: 118-505 (£2 per minute)
US Consulate and Embassy: tel. 020/7499-9000, Mon–Fri 8:30–17:00 (24 Grosvenor Square, Tube: Bond Street, www.usembassy.org.uk)
Canadian High Commission: tel. 020/7258-6600, passport services available Mon–Fri 9:30–13:30 (38 Grosvenor Street, Tube: Bond Street, www.unitedkingdom.gc.ca)
Toll-Free Numbers: Any number that begins with 0800 (but not others, such as 0845 or 0870) is toll-free.

your smartphone cheaply is to disable data roaming entirely, and avoid going online with it until you have free Wi-Fi (e.g. in a café or at your hotel).

For more on the fast-changing world of telephones, talk to your service provider or see www.ricksteves.com/phoning.

Internet

Many hotels offer some form of free or cheap Internet access—either a computer in the lobby or Wi-Fi in the room (for use with your own mobile device or laptop). Otherwise, your hotelier can point you to the nearest Internet café. If you're bringing your own mobile device, Wi-Fi hotspots are plentiful. Consider signing up with The Cloud, a free Wi-Fi service found in many convenient spots, including London train stations, museums, coffee shops, cafés, and shopping centers (www.thecloud.net/free-wifi; use your hotel's street address to sign up). Within Tube stations, free Wi-Fi is limited to transit info, but you can pay for all-purpose Wi-Fi with a credit card (http://my.virginmedia.com/wifi). Some useful London-specific smartphone apps (that work even when you're not online) are: MX Apps free Tube map, City Maps 2Go for London ($2), and Time Out London's free "Things to Do" app. If you've got the software, you can make phone calls to other computers and telephones inexpensively or even free using Skype (www.skype.com), Google Talk (www.google.com/talk), or Facetime (preloaded on many Apple devices).

SIGHTSEEING TIPS

Sightseeing Passes: Unlike some other cities, London does not offer a must-have sightseeing pass guaranteed to save you time and money. However, the London Pass can be worthwhile for rabid sightseers, covering lots of pricey big-name sights and letting you skip the line. To see if it works for you, check the list of included sights and do the math at www .londonpass.com.

Avoiding Lines with Advance Tickets: At some sights, you can skip ticket-buying lines by buying in advance, either online or at a less-crowded location. I mention these in my sights listings.

Hours: Hours of sights can change unexpectedly; confirm the latest times on the sight's website or www.visitlondon.com. Many sights stop admitting people 30–60 minutes before closing time, and guards start shooing people out before the actual closing time, so don't save the best for last.

Typical Rules: A few important sights such as the Halls of Parliament have metal detectors or conduct bag searches that will slow your entry. Others might require you to check (for free) daypacks and coats.

Photos and videos are normally allowed, but flashes or tripods usually are not. Many sights offer guided tours and rent audioguides (£3–5). Most have an on-site café. Expect changes—artwork can be in restoration, displayed elsewhere, or on tour.

Discounts: Many sights offer "concessions" (or "concs") for seniors, children, families, and students. It's worth asking.

Late Hours: At least one London sight is open late every night, to extend your sightseeing day. ✪ See the sidebar on page 149.

Free Rick Steves Audio Tours: I've produced free audio tours of many of London's best sights. With an iPod (or other MP3 player) or a smartphone, you can tour the British Museum, British Library, St. Paul's Cathedral, the City, and the Westminster neighborhood. Download them from iTunes, Google Play, or from www.ricksteves.com.

Theft and Emergencies

Theft: While violent crime is rare in the city center, the Artful Dodger is alive and well in London. Be on guard against pickpockets, particularly on public transportation and in places crowded with tourists. I wear a money belt. Dial 999 for the police.

Affording London's Sights

Free Museums: The British Museum, British Library, National Gallery, National Portrait Gallery, Tate Britain, Tate Modern, Wallace Collection, Imperial War Museum, Victoria and Albert Museum, Natural History Museum, Science Museum, National Army Museum, Sir John Soane's Museum, and the Museum of London.

Free Churches: Most churches are free. Even the big churches charging admission—Westminster Abbey and St. Paul's—offer free evensong services daily.

Other Freebies: Changing of the Guard, rants at Speaker's Corner, Harrods, Old Bailey, and Houses of Parliament. There are lunch concerts at St. Martin-in-the-Fields (www.smitf.org) and summertime movies at The Scoop amphitheater (see www.morelondon.com). For other freebies, check out www.freelondonlistings.co.uk.

Sightseeing Deals: Paper train tickets can get you same-day two-for-one discounts at the London Eye, Tower of London, Tate Modern, and Madame Tussauds Waxworks. See www.daysoutguide.co.uk.

Theater: Compared with Broadway's prices, London theater is a bargain. The freestanding "tkts" booth at Leicester Square gets you up to 50 percent off, and there are even cheaper seats bought directly from theater box offices.

Medical Help: In Britain, dial 999 for a medical emergency. For minor ailments, do as the Brits do and go to a pharmacist (a "chemist"), where qualified technicians routinely diagnose and prescribe. Or ask at your hotel for help; they know of the nearest medical and emergency services. Local hospitals have good-quality 24-hour emergency care centers where any tourist can drop in. St. Thomas's Hospital, immediately across the river from Big Ben, has a fine reputation.

ACTIVITIES

Nightlife and Entertainment

London bubbles with top-notch entertainment seven days a week: plays, movie premieres, concerts, Gilbert and Sullivan, tango lessons, stand-up, Baha'i meetings, walking tours, shopping, museums open late, and the endlessly entertaining pub scene. Perhaps your best entertainment is just to take the Tube to Leicester Square on a pleasant evening, and explore the bustling West End. The two best sources for what's on are *Time Out* magazine (£3, sold everywhere, www.timeout.com) and the TI's free monthly *London Planner*.

Theater (a.k.a. "Theatre")

London's theater rivals Broadway's in quality and usually beats it in price. Choose from 200 offerings—Shakespeare, glitzy musicals, sex farces, serious chamber drama, cutting-edge fringe, revivals starring movie celebs, and more. London does it all well. Along with the trendiest plays, you'll always find a number of well-executed perennials: *Phantom of the Opera, Chicago, Les Misérables, The Lion King,* and so on. To see what's showing, pick up the *Official London Theatre Guide* (free at hotels and box offices) or check www.officiallondontheatre.co.uk.

Buying Tickets: Performances are generally every night except Sunday, usually with one or two matinees a week. Tickets range from about £15 to £60.

Buy in person from the theater box office (no booking fee), or order by phone (some charge booking fee) or online from the theater's website (£2-3 booking fee). Other easy online sites (which charge similar booking fees) are www.ticketmaster.co.uk and www.seetickets.com. Ticket agencies, located in offices around London, can be convenient but generally charge a 25 percent fee above the face value.

The famous half-price "tkts" booth at Leicester Square sells discounted tickets for top-price seats to less-in-demand shows—but only on the day of the performance. Lines often form early, and there's a £3 service charge. Half-price tickets can be a good deal, unless you want the cheapest (balcony) seats or the hottest shows. The "tkts" booth is open Monday through Saturday 10:00–19:00, Sunday 11:00–16:00. Check the day's list of available shows at www.tkts.co.uk.

Cheap Tricks: Most theaters offer discounted tickets, called "concessions," or "concs." These can be for matinee performances, standing-room, restricted view seats (behind a pillar), senior/student deals, or tickets returned at the last minute. Buying from scalpers on the street can, like anywhere, get you a good deal or a worthless forgery. Many theaters are so small that there's hardly a bad seat. Bold theatergoers buy cheap tickets, then—as the lights begin to dim—scoot up to a better seat. You wouldn't be the only one rustling in the dark. Shakespeare did it.

Most theaters are found in the West End, between Piccadilly and Covent Garden, especially along Shaftesbury Avenue. Shakespeare's Globe (on the South Bank) presents a full repertoire May through September in a thatched, open-air replica of the Bard's original theater. The £5 "groundling" tickets—standing-room at the foot of the stage—are most fun (tel. 020/7401-9919, www.shakespearesglobe.com).

Classical Music

Concerts at Historic Churches: Check for free-or-cheap classical music offered many weekdays around 13:00 at St. Bride's Church (Tube: St. Paul's, tel. 020/7427-0133, www.stbrides.com), St. James's at Piccadilly (Tube: Piccadilly, tel. 020/7381-0441, www.st-james-piccadilly.org), and St. Martin-in-the-Fields on Trafalgar Square (tel. 020/7766-1100, www.smitf.org). St. Martin-in-the-Fields also hosts fine evening concerts by candlelight and Wednesday jazz. Evensong services are held at St. Paul's Cathedral (Tue–Sat at 17:00, Sun at 15:15), Westminster Abbey (Mon–Fri at 17:00, except spoken—not sung—on Wed, Sat–Sun at 15:00 except June–Sept, when it's 17:00 on Sat, organ recitals Sun 17:45), and Southwark Cathedral (Tube: London Bridge, Mon–Fri at 17:30, Sat at 16:00, Sun at 15:00).

Opera and Dance: Some of the world's best opera is belted out at the prestigious Royal Opera House, near Covent Garden (tel. 020/7304-4000, www.roh.org.uk), and at the London Coliseum near Leicester Square (English National Opera, toll tel. 0871-911-0200, www.eno.org). For dance, try Sadler's Wells Theatre (Tube: Angel, tel. 020/7863-8198, www.sadlerswells.com).

Seasonal London

Summer Fun: There are plays under the stars at leafy Regent's Park (Tube: Baker Street, toll tel. 0844-826-4242, www.openairtheatre.org). Royal Albert Hall hosts "Promenade" classical music concerts, where peasants can score cheap standing-room tickets (Tube: South Kensington, toll tel. 0845-401-5045, www.bbc.co.uk/proms).

On the South Bank, stroll the Jubilee Walkway along the Thames, from the London Eye to Tower Bridge, past pubs and cafés, the British Film Institute Southbank cinema (tel. 020/7928-3232, check www.bfi .org.uk for schedules), and Shakespeare's Globe. The Scoop, an outdoor amphitheater next to City Hall and Tower Bridge hosts outdoor movies, concerts, dance, and theater—almost nightly and usually free (www.more london.com).

Winter Diversions: From late November to early January, London is dressed in its Victorian Christmas best. Trafalgar Square erects a Christmas tree, and outdoor ice rinks emerge at Somerset House and the Tower of London. Store windows glitter along Oxford Street, Bond Street, Regent Street, and Brompton Road. Father Christmas is in his grotto at Harrods (Tube: Knightsbridge) and Selfridges (Tube: Bond Street). Hyde Park stages a kitschy carnival (www.hydeparkwinter wonderland.com). Take in a family-fun holiday play called a "panto," or pantomime (try www.hackneyempire.co.uk or www.oldvictheatre.com). On the South Bank, nibble your way through Christmas markets at the Borough Market (Tube: London Bridge) or the German-flavored Market (Tube: Waterloo, www.xmas-markets.com). Finally, join thousands of revelers on Trafalgar Square to watch fireworks from the London Eye to ring in the New Year.

Tours

▲▲▲**Hop-on, Hop-off Double-Decker Bus Tours:** For a grand and efficient intro to London, ride through the city on an open-air bus past the main sights, while you listen to commentary. Hop on at any of the 30 stops along the two-hour loop, pay as you board, ride awhile, hop off to sightsee, then catch the next bus (10-20 minutes later) to carry on. Some routes have good live guides, while others have mediocre recorded commentary.

Several similar companies offer several different routes. Pick up their brochures or check online for the various options, extras, and discounts. **Big Bus London Tours** tend to have more dynamic guides and more frequent buses (£30, tel. 020/7233-9533, www.bigbustours.com). Original **London Sightseeing Bus Tour** is cheaper and nearly as good (£28, £4 Rick Steves discount for two with this book—raise bloody hell if they won't honor it, tel. 020/8877-1722, www.theoriginaltour.com). **London by Night** offers a bare-bones but atmospheric twilight circuit (£19, tel. 020/8545-6109, www.london-by-night.net).

▲▲Walking Tours: Top-notch, highly-entertaining local guides lead groups on two-hour tours through specific slices of London's past. Choose from the world of Charles Dickens, Harry Potter, the Plague, Shakespeare, Legal London, the Beatles, the ever-popular Jack the Ripper, plus many others. To see what's available, look for brochures, check *Time Out* magazine, or contact the various companies directly. To take a walking tour, you simply show up at the announced location and pay the guide (usually cash only).

London Walks has a wide and fascinating repertoire of tours led by professional guides and actors (£9, tel. 020/7624-3978, recorded info 020/7624-9255, www.walks.com). The **Essential London Walk** offers a low-budget, high-quality highlights tour of the historic core (£6 for my readers, 365 days a year, just show up at 10:00 at the Eros statue on Piccadilly Circus, www.guidelondon.org.uk). **Sandemans New London** has a free, irreverent, youth-oriented tour of the basic sights (tours are free, but a tip is definitely expected, www.newlondon-tours.com).

Private Guides: If you'd like your own personal tour guide, standard rates for registered Blue Badge guides are about £135–160 for four hours, and £200 or more for nine hours (tel. 020/7611-2545, www.touristguides.org.uk or www.britainsbestguides.org). For a personal guide who can also drive you around London (£450/day) try www.driverguidetours.com or http://seeitinstyle.synthasite.com.

Bike Tours: Though London traffic is pretty intense to navigate on your own, consider a guided bike tour. **London Bicycle Tour Company** rents to individuals (£3.50/hour, £20/day) and leads tours (£19, includes bike) on three different routes (located at 1a Gabriel's Wharf on the South Bank, Tube: Waterloo, tel. 020/7928-6838, www.londonbicycle.com). **Fat Tire Bike Tours** offers two different itineraries (£20–30, mobile 078-8233-8779, www.fattirebiketourslondon.com). Anyone with a credit card can rent a **Barclays Cycle** bike from a streetside station.

▲▲Thames Cruises: Several boat companies ply the Thames, useful for either a relaxing guided cruise or for point-A-to-B travel around London. The handiest boats leave from Westminster Pier (near Big Ben) and Waterloo Pier (near the London Eye). Some helpful stops for sightseers are: Bankside (Shakespeare's Globe), Blackfriars (St. Paul's), London Bridge, and Tower of London. Farther afield, boats go to Greenwich and

Jack the Ripper

In 1888 locals were terrorized by the murder of five prostitutes within a few weeks. In the wee hours, the murderer slit the throats and cut out the guts of his victims in the poor and wretched side of town. These were desperate women—so desperate they took their customers not to a bed, but up against a wall for a "four-penny knee trembler."

Little remains from the Ripper's world (roughly around Tube: Aldgate East), but that doesn't stop local guides from spinning a great story. They take you by the Ten Bells Pub (est. 1753), the hangout of one of the victims. Across the street is Christ Church, whose chiming bells helped many Ripper witnesses pinpoint the time of the crimes. Nearby Fournier Street still has many of the old brick tenement houses that filled this once-dreary, soot-covered neighborhood.

Jack the Ripper got his nickname from the tabloids, which made a fortune on this sensational story. The killer was never found.

the Docklands (to the east), and Kew Gardens and Hampton Court to the west.

From Westminster Pier, **City Cruises** is handy to the Tower of London and Greenwich (£9 one-way, £15.50 all-day pass, tel. 020/7740-0400, www.citycruises.com), and so is the similar **Thames River Services** (tel. 020/7930-4097, www.thamesriverservices.co.uk). **Crown River Services** has a hop-on, hop-off "Circular Cruise" route (£3 to go one stop, £11 round-trip, tel. 020/7936-2033, www.crownriver.com).

From Waterloo Pier, **Thames Clippers** is more like an express commuter bus than a tour cruise, traveling fast and making all the stops along the way (£6 single trip, £13.60 all-day, tel. 020/7001-2222, www.thames clippers.com).

Buy tickets at the docks. Some companies give discounts for the Tube's TravelCard and Oyster card, and for children and seniors—it's worth asking.

London Duck Tours takes 30 tourists on goofy-but-fun tours on amphibious vehicles. You drive past Big Ben and other sights before splashing into the Thames for a cruise (£21, departs from near London Eye, tel. 020/7928-3132, www.londonducktours.co.uk).

Shopping

London is great for shoppers—and, thanks to the high prices, perhaps even better for window-shoppers. In the 1960s, London set the tone for Mod clothing, and it's been a major fashion capital ever since.

Most stores are open Monday through Saturday from roughly 10:00 to 18:00, and many close Sundays. Large department stores stay open until 20:00 or 21:00. For one-stop shopping for essential items, try large chain stores such as Marks & Spencer (www.marksandspencer.com).

West End High Fashion: You'll find big-name fashion stores along Regent Street (between Oxford Circus and Piccadilly), old-fashioned gentlemen's stores on Jermyn Street, bookstores along Charing Cross Road, and more boutiques around Covent Garden. All these are part of the West End Walk (✪ see page 61).

Harrods and "Harvey Nick's": Near Hyde Park, you'll find London's most famous and touristy department store, Harrods. With more than four acres of retail space covering seven floors, it has everything from elephants to toothbrushes, from artisan cheese to a £10,000 toy car. Harrods' Georgian Restaurant serves an elegant afternoon tea. The store has also become famous for its Egyptian theme and memorials to Princess Diana, but those were the pet projects of Harrods' former owner, and the store came under new management in 2010. The nearby Beauchamp Place is lined with classy and fascinating shops (Mon–Sat 10:00–20:00, Sun 11:30–18:00, located on Brompton Road, Tube: Knightsbridge, tel. 020/7730-1234, www.harrods.com).

A few blocks away is Harvey Nichols. Once Princess Diana's favorite (and now serving Kate Middleton), "Harvey Nick's" remains the department store du jour (Mon–Sat 10:00–20:00, Sun 12:00–18:00, near Harrods, 109–125 Knightsbridge, Tube: Knightsbridge, tel. 020/7235-5000, www.harveynichols.com).

Street Markets: London's weekend flea markets are legendary, and there are early-morning produce markets any day of the week. Covent Garden's daily market is handy to other sightseeing (open daily 10:00–18:30, tel. 020-7836-9136, www.coventgardenlife.com).

Portobello Road Market is the classic London street market. On Saturdays, this funky-yet-quaint Notting Hill street of pastel-painted houses and offbeat antiques shops is enlivened even more with 2,000 additional stalls. Antiques, produce, garage-sale items, food stands, live music, and huge crowds create a festival atmosphere. On non-Saturdays, the

Practicalities

street itself is fun to explore. (The market is Sat 5:30–17:00, on Sundays everything is closed, Tube: Notting Hill Gate, tel. 020/7229-8354, www.portobelloroad.co.uk.)

Camden Lock Market in north London is a huge, trendy, youth-oriented arts-and-crafts festival. It runs daily 10:00–18:00, but is busiest on weekends (Tube: Camden Town, 020/7485-7963, www.camdenlock market.com).

For a pleasant Sunday in the East End, take the Tube to Liverpool Street and visit the huge, covered Spitalfields Market (shops open daily 11:00–19:00, tel. 020/7375-2963, www.visitspitalfields.com). Then walk to the Petticoat Lane Market (Wentworth Street) and Backyard Market in the heart of the "Banglatown" Bangladeshi community (Sat and Sun only, www.backyardmarket.co.uk).

Auction Houses: London's famous auctioneers welcome the curious public Monday through Friday for viewing and bidding. Contact Sotheby's (34–35 New Bond Street, Tube: Oxford Circus, tel. 020/7293-5000, www.sothebys.com) or Christie's (8 King Street, Tube: Green Park, tel. 020/7839-9060, www.christies.com).

Sizes: British clothing sizes are different from the US. For example, a woman's size 10 dress (US) is a UK size 14, and a size 8 woman's shoe (US) is a UK size 5½.

Getting a VAT Refund: If you purchase more than £30 worth of goods at a single store, you may be eligible to get a refund of the 20 percent Value-Added Tax (VAT). It's easiest through a VAT-refund service such as Premier Tax Free (www.premiertaxfree.com) or Global Blue (www.global-blue.com), which have offices at major airports. For more details, see www.ricksteves.com/vat.

Customs for American Shoppers: You are allowed to take home $800 worth of items per person duty-free, once every 30 days. You can also bring in duty-free a liter of alcohol.

As for food, you can take home many processed and packaged foods (e.g. vacuum-packed cheeses, chocolate, mustard) but no fresh produce or meats. Any liquid-containing foods must be packed in checked luggage, a potential recipe for disaster. To check customs rules and duty rates, visit www.cbp.gov.

www.ricksteves.com

This Pocket guide is one of more than 30 titles in my series of guidebooks on European travel. I also produce a public television series, *Rick Steves' Europe,* and a public radio show, *Travel with Rick Steves.* My website, www.ricksteves.com, offers free travel information, free vodcasts and podcasts of my shows, free audio tours of Europe's great sights, a Graffiti Wall for travelers' comments, guidebook updates, my travel blog, an online travel store, and information on European railpasses and our tours of Europe.

How Was Your Trip? If you'd like to share your tips, concerns, and discoveries after using this book, please fill out the survey at www.rick steves.com/feedback. It helps us and fellow travelers. Cheers!

British–Yankee Vocabulary

afters–dessert

anticlockwise–counterclockwise

bangers and mash–sausage and mashed potatoes

bloody–damn

blow off–fart

bobby–policeman ("the Bill" is more common)

Bob's your uncle–there you go (with a shrug), naturally

boffin–nerd, geek

bollocks–testicles (used in many colorful expressions)

bolshy–argumentative

bubble and squeak–cabbage and potatoes fried together

bum–butt

cheers–good-bye or thanks; also a toast

chemist–pharmacist

chippie–fish-and-chip shop; carpenter (see also "joiner")

chock-a-block–jam-packed

chuffed–pleased

concs (pronounced "conks")–short for "concession," or discount

crisps–potato chips

cuppa–cup of tea

curry–any Indian meal flavored with curry, popular with all Brits

dear–expensive

donkey's years–ages, long time

dummy–pacifier

elevenses–coffee-and-biscuits break before lunch

fag–cigarette

fagged–exhausted

faggot–meatball

fairy cake–cupcake

fancy–to like, to be attracted to (a person)

fanny–vagina

first floor–second floor

fizzy drink–pop or soda

flat–apartment

Frogs–French people

full Monty–whole shebang; everything

geezer–dude (slang for young man)

green fingers–green thumbs

grizzle–grumble, fuss (especially by a baby)

gutted–deeply disappointed

half eight–8:30 (not 7:30)

hash sign–pound sign, as on a phone

hen night–bachelorette party

holiday–vacation

homely–homey or cozy

ice lolly–Popsicle

Joe Bloggs–John Q. Public

jumble sale–rummage sale

just a tick–just a second

knackered–exhausted (Cockney: cream crackered)

knickers–ladies' panties

ladybird–ladybug

left luggage–baggage check

let–rent, as in property

licenced–restaurant authorized to sell alcohol

lie-in, having a–sleeping in late

lift–elevator

loo–toilet or bathroom

lorry–truck

Practicalities

mac–mackintosh raincoat

Marmite–yeast paste, spread on sandwiches

mate–buddy (boy or girl)

mews–former stables converted to two-story rowhouses (London)

moggie–cat

naff–dorky

natter–talk on and on

noughts & crosses–tic-tac-toe

off-licence–liquor store

on offer–for sale

pants–underwear, briefs

pear-shaped–messed up, gone wrong

petrol–gas

pissed, paralytic, bevvied, wellied, popped up, merry, trollied, ratted, rat-arsed, pissed as a newt–drunk

public school–private "prep" school (e.g., Eton)

pudding–dessert in general

pull, to be on the–looking for love

punter–customer, especially in gambling

quid–a pound (money)

randy–horny

ring up–call (telephone)

rubber–eraser

rubbish–bad

serviette–napkin

shag–intercourse (cruder than in the US)

smalls–underwear

snogging–kissing, making out

sod–mildly offensive insult

sod it, sod off–screw it, screw off

spend a penny–urinate

stag night–bachelor party

starkers–buck naked

stone–14 pounds (weight)

stroppy–bad-tempered

subway–underground walkway

ta–thank you

tatty–worn out or tacky

telly–TV

tenner–£10 bill

tight as a fish's bum–cheapskate (watertight)

top hole–first rate

top up–refill a drink

torch–flashlight

twee–quaint, cute

twitcher–bird watcher

way out–exit

wee (adj)–small (Scottish)

Wellingtons, wellies–rubber boots

whacked–exhausted

whinge (rhymes with hinge)–whine

wind up–tease, irritate

witter on–gab and gab

yob–hooligan

zed–the letter Z

INDEX

PHOTO CREDITS

Title Page
© sborisov/123rf.com

Table of Contents
Left © Claudio Divizia/123rf.com, right © Karel Miragaya/123rf.com

Introduction
Images © Cameron Hewitt, Rick Steves

Westminster Walk
p. 28 © Tadeusz Ibrom/123rf.com; other images © Dominic Bonuccelli, Rick Steves, Cameron Hewitt, Gene Openshaw

Westminster Abbey Tour
p. 33, left © Michael Jenner / Alamy; p. 33, right © Angelo Hornak / Alamy; p. 35, left © Lightworks Media / Alamy; p. 35, right © ImageState / Alamy; p. 38, left © Peter Spirer /Dreamstime.com; p. 38, right © travelib europe / Alamy; other image © Rick Steves

National Gallery Tour
p. 39 © 123rf.com; p. 42, left, The Yorck Project*, commons.wikimedia.org; p. 42, right, The Yorck Project*, commons.wikimedia.org; p. 45 © The Art Gallery Collection/Alamy; p. 47, left, The Yorck Project*, commons.wikimedia.org; p. 48 © INTERFOTO / Alamy; p. 50, left, The Yorck Project*, commons.wikimedia.org; p. 52, left, The Yorck Project*, commons.wikimedia.org; p. 53, left, The Yorck Project*, commons.wikimedia.org; p. 55, left, The Yorck Project*, commons.wikimedia.org; p. 57, © INTERFOTO / Alamy; p. 59, © John Baran / Alamy; p. 60 © The Art Gallery Collection/Alamy

West End Walk
p. 68 © Patrickwang /Dreamstime.com; other images © Gene Openshaw, Cameron Hewitt

British Museum Tour
p. 74 © jorisov/123rf.com; p. 75 © Björn Höglund/123rf.com; p. 81, left, © Frankie Roberto/flickr.com; p. 81, right © Marcus Cyron, (Scan) (ISBN 978-3-8228-5455-6), commons.wikimedia.org; p. 82, left, Mario Sánchez Prada/flickr.com; p. 83, left © commons.wikimedia.org; p. 83, right, © Keith Schengili-Roberts; p. 86, left, © Beren Patterson / Alamy; p. 89 © Beren Patterson / Alamy; p. 90 © Erin Babnik / Alamy; p. 94 © Mike Peel (www.mikepeel.net), Creative Commons CC-BY-SA-2.5; other images © Rick Steves, Gene Openshaw, Jennifer Hauseman, David C. Hoerlein

British Library Tour
p. 102 © Rob Ford/ Dreamstime.com; p. 103 © Alistair Scott /Dreamstime.com; p. 109, left © All Rights Reserved. The British Library Board. Licence Number: AVATRA01; p. 111 © All Rights Reserved. The British Library Board. Licence Number: AVATRA01; p. 113, left, Schoenberg Center for Electronic Text & Image (SCETI), commons.wikimedia .org; other images © Cameron Hewitt, Gene Openshaw

St. Paul's Tour

p. 115 © Anthony Baggett/Dreamstime.com; p. 119 © Jeff Gynane/123rf.com; p. 122, right © Angelo Hornak / Alamy; p. 124, left © Martin Chalifour photos; other images © Cameron Hewitt, Rick Steves, Gene Openshaw

Tower of London Tour

p. 136, right, © ImageState / Alamy; other images © Rick Steves, Gene Openshaw, Jennifer Hauseman, Dominic Bonuccelli

Sights

p. 140 © Elena Elisseeva/123rf.com; other image © Dominic Bonuccelli

Sleeping

Images © Cameron Hewitt, Rick Steves

Eating

p. 188 © Baloncici/123rf.com; ; p. 189 © Elena Rostunova /Dreamstime.com; other image © Lauren Mills

Practicalities

p. 210 © Elena Elisseeva/123rf.com; other image © Cameron Hewitt

* Additional Yorck Project information: The work of art depicted in this image and the reproduction thereof are in the public domain worldwide. The reproduction is part of a collection of reproductions compiled by The Yorck Project. The compilation copyright is held by Zenodot Verlagsgesellschaft mbH and licensed under the GNU Free Documentation License. The Yorck Project: 10.000 Meisterwerke der Malerei. DVD-ROM, 2002. ISBN 3936122202. Distributed by DIRECTMEDIA Publishing GmbH.

Unless otherwise noted, copyrights apply to photographs of artwork.

Audio Europe™

Rick's Free Travel App

Get your FREE **Rick Steves Audio Europe**™ app to enjoy…

- Dozens of self-guided tours of Europe's top museums, sights and historic walks
- Hundreds of tracks filled with cultural insights and sightseeing tips from Rick's radio interviews
- All organized into handy geographic playlists
- For iPhone, iPad, iPod Touch, Android

With Rick whispering in your ear, Europe gets even better.

Find out more at ricksteves.com

Join a Rick Steves tour

Enjoy Europe's warmest welcome... with the flexibility and friendship of a small group getting to know Rick's favorite places and people. It all starts with our free tour catalog and DVD.

Great guides, small groups, no grumps.

See more than three dozen itineraries throughout Europe
tours.ricksteves.com

Start your trip at

Free information and great gear to

▸ Plan Your Trip

Browse thousands of articles and a wealth of money-saving tips for planning your dream trip. You'll find up-to-date information on Europe's best destinations, packing smart, getting around, finding rooms, staying healthy, avoiding scams and more.

▸ Eurail Passes

Find out, step-by-step, if a railpass makes sense for your trip—and how to avoid buying more than you need. Get a bunch of free extras!

▸ Graffiti Wall & Travelers Helpline

Learn, ask, share—our online community of savvy travelers is a great resource for first-time travelers to Europe, as well as seasoned pros.

Rick Steves' Europe Through the Back Door, Inc.

ricksteves.com

turn your travel dreams into affordable reality

▶ Rick's Free Audio Europe™ App

The Rick Steves Audio Europe™ app brings history and art to life. Enjoy Rick's audio tours of Europe's top museums, sights and neighborhood walks—plus hundreds of tracks including travel tips and cultural insights from Rick's radio show—all organized into geographic playlists. Learn more at ricksteves.com.

▶ Great Gear from Rick's Travel Store

Pack light and right—on a budget—with Rick's custom-designed carry-on bags, wheeled bags, day packs, travel accessories, guidebooks, journals, maps and Blu-ray/DVDs of his TV shows.

130 Fourth Avenue North, PO Box 2009 • Edmonds, WA 98020 USA
Phone: (425) 771-8303 • Fax: (425) 771-0833 • www.ricksteves.com

Rick Steves®   www.ricksteves.com

NOW AVAILABLE:
eBOOKS, DVD & BLU-RAY

eBOOKS

Nearly all Rick Steves guides are available as eBooks. Check with your favorite bookseller.

RICK STEVES' EUROPE DVDS

10 New Shows 2011–2012
Austria & the Alps
Eastern Europe
England & Wales
European Christmas
European Travel Skills & Specials
France
Germany, BeNeLux & More
Greece & Turkey
Iran
Ireland & Scotland
Italy's Cities
Italy's Countryside
Scandinavia
Spain
Travel Extras

BLU-RAY

Celtic Charms
Eastern Europe Favorites
European Christmas
Italy Through the Back Door
Mediterranean Mosaic
Surprising Cities of Europe

PHRASE BOOKS & DICTIONARIES

French
French, Italian & German
German
Italian
Portuguese
Spanish

JOURNALS

Rick Steves' Pocket Travel Journal
Rick Steves' Travel Journal

PLANNING MAPS

Britain, Ireland & London
Europe
France & Paris
Germany, Austria & Switzerland
Ireland
Italy
Spain & Portugal

Rick Steves guidebooks are published by Avalon Travel, a member of the Perseus Books Group.
Rick Steves books and DVDs are available at bookstores and through online booksellers.

Avalon Travel
a member of the Perseus Books Group
1700 Fourth Street
Berkeley, CA 94710

Text © 2013, 2012, 2011 by Rick Steves.
Maps © 2013 by Europe Through the Back Door. All rights reserved.
Underground Map © 2012, 2011, 2010, 2009, 2008, 2007, 2006 Transport for
London. Registered User No. 09/1498/P. Used with permission.

Printed in China by R.R. Donnelley.
Updated for fifth printing April 2013.
Sixth printing September 2013.

ISBN 978-1-59880-380-8
ISSN 2159-6794

For the latest on Rick's lectures, books, tours, public radio show, and public television series, contact Europe Through the Back Door, Box 2009, Edmonds, WA
98020, tel. 425/771-8303, fax 425/771-0833, www.ricksteves.com, rick@rickste-
ves.com.

ETBD Managing Editor: Risa Laib
Avalon Travel Senior Editor and Series Manager: Madhu Prasher
Avalon Travel Project Editor: Kevin McLain
Copy Editor: Judith Brown
Proofreader: Nikki Ioakimedes
Indexer: Stephen Callahan
Production & Typesetting: McGuire Barber Design
Cover Design: Kimberly Glyder Design
Interior Design: Darren Alessi
Graphic Content Director: Laura VanDeventer
Maps and Graphics: David C. Hoerlein, Laura VanDeventer, Lauren Mills, Barb
Geisler, Mike Morgenfeld, Brice Ticen, Kat Bennett
Cover Photos: Yeoman warders © Janet Gill/Getty Images; Millennium Wheel
© Charles Bowman/Getty Images

*Although the authors and publisher have made every effort to provide up-to-date
information, they accept no responsibility for loss, injury, mushy peas, or inconve-
nience sustained by any person using this book.*

ABOUT THE AUTHORS

Rick Steves

Since 1973, Rick Steves has spent 100 days every year exploring Europe. Along with writing and researching a bestselling series of guidebooks, Rick produces a public television series *(Rick Steves' Europe)*, a public radio show *(Travel with Rick Steves)*, and an app and podcast *(Rick Steves Audio Europe)*; writes a nationally syndicated newspaper column; organizes guided tours that take over ten thousand travelers to Europe annually; and offers an information-packed website (www.ricksteves.com). With the help of his hardworking staff of 80 at Europe Through the Back Door—in Edmonds, Washington, just north of Seattle—Rick's mission is to make European travel fun, affordable, and culturally enlightening for Americans.

Connect with Rick:

facebook.com/RickSteves twitter: @RickSteves

Gene Openshaw

Gene Openshaw is a writer, composer, tour guide, and lecturer on art and history. Specializing in writing walking tours of Europe's cultural sights, Gene has co-authored ten of Rick's books and contributes to Rick's public television series. As a composer, Gene has written a full-length opera *(Matter)*, a violin sonata, and dozens of songs. He lives near Seattle with his daughter, and roots for the Mariners in good times and bad.

FOLDOUT COLOR MAP

The foldout map on the opposite page includes:
• A map of London on one side
• Maps of the London Underground, Greater London, and England on the other side